MY MORNING
WALKS
WITH GOD

A DAILY DEVOTIONAL

A Six Month Journey Filled with
Reflections, Revelations and Recollections

GREG A. LANE

My Morning Walk with God

ISBN 978-0-9984882-0-2

Copyright © 2017 Greg A. Lane
Website: MyMorningWalksWithGod.com

Published by Inspired Design & Graphics

PREFACE

In the early 1990s I noticed that my wife, Lisa, would take time out of her busy day, sometimes daily, to jot down her thoughts and feelings in a journal. I secretly admired the discipline she had in writing down the things that were in her heart, and often wished that I could do the same. You see, I had my own personal reflections and revelations that I thought were noteworthy, but frankly, I was somewhat lazy and undisciplined, refusing to take time to sit down and put pen to paper.

That changed in 2009 when I determined within myself to start a daily discipline of writing my thoughts down to share with others. It was not a coincidence that in that very same year I began another much-needed discipline in my life... a daily morning walk of about 2 miles. It was during those early morning walks that I began the most needed and most important discipline of all... a time of daily communion with the Lord. I prayed and listened to His voice on the inside of me each morning. Those moments spent communing with Him during my morning walk became the springboard for all of the writings in this book. Almost every entry was written immediately after returning home from "My Morning Walks with God"... thus, the name for the book.

It is my hope that many will read this book and use it as part of their daily discipline in seeking God in their own personal "Morning WALK with God."

BEFORE YOU READ...

I'd like to offer an explanation about the way this book is presented and laid out. First, you will notice that each devotional has two dates at the top of the page. This has been done for those who wish to incorporate this devotional into a six-month reading plan.

Secondly, at the end of most pages you will find random thoughts and revelations in the form of *Wisdom Nuggets, Words of Encouragement,* and *Food for Thought.* These are "bonus" thoughts for each day and not necessarily a continuing thought from the devotional. These little "Nuggets" were also received during my *Morning Walks with God.* You will find that many of these thoughts focus on the meanings of words that we often use but don't always fully comprehend. It is amazing how often we use words that we think we understand, only to discover that deeper meanings exist that we've completely overlooked. Revelation is experienced when the deeper meanings are found!

One final note: There are dozens of ways to put emphasis on words that are written on a page. My favorite way is using all capital letters. You will find hundreds of instances of this within the following pages. So, anytime you see words in "all caps" please PAY ATTENTION.

May you be blessed as you read this devotional and incorporate it into your own personal daily discipline of WALKING WITH GOD.

Micah 6:8
He hath shewed thee, O man, what is good; and what doth the LORD require of thee, but to do justly, and to love mercy, and to WALK HUMBLY WITH THY GOD?

REFLECTORS
January 1 | July 1

I woke up rather early one autumn morning for my regular morning prayer walk. The sun had not yet risen, yet I could see the detailed outlines of my shadow on the ground. How could this be possible?! A brilliant full moon was overhead that morning... bright enough to cast a shadow upon the ground. As a matter of fact, as the sun began to rise that morning the moon was still brilliantly bright even up until 6:30am. But, when the sun had completely risen, the brilliance of the moon, though still visible in the sky, could barely be seen because of the radiance of the sun.

Christians are called to be LIGHT in a dark world. But the light that we dispense is not our own. It is a reflection of the SON. Many times we misunderstand this. We think just because people can see the light within us that we're something special. Lucifer (meaning "Light-bearer" by translation) thought that he was something special because of his radiance. Isaiah 14:12 refers to him as a "shining star" and "son of the morning." But, he forgot that he was only a reflector of the True Light. Because of his pride, the "Light-Bearer" became the "Prince of Darkness." His light was snuffed out. May we never forget that, especially in these DARK days. You see, the SON is about to RISE and He will not share His glory with another. Yes, we are called to be LIGHTS in this world, but always be prepared for the moment when the SON shows up on the scene to shine with His rightful glory. Our lights will then pale in comparison!

1 Corinthians 15:41
There is one glory of the sun, and another glory of the moon, and another glory of the stars: for one star differeth from another star in glory.

Philippians 2:15
That ye may be blameless and harmless, the sons of God, without rebuke, in the midst of a crooked and perverse nation, among whom ye shine as lights in the world;

TODAY'S FOOD FOR THOUGHT
Which will hold more... a metal container or one that's made out of pliable rubber? The rubber container, right? Why? Because it will stretch in order to accommodate more content. The same holds true for you and me. The more we're willing to be stretched the more we are able to contain. *STRETCH ME, Lord!*

MARY'S FAVORITE PLACE
January 2 | July 2

If you like doing a little detective work then you might enjoy this. I was reading my Bible one morning and came across a scripture reference about a woman named Mary who was a follower of Jesus. I don't usually go off on tangents, but I noticed something this particular morning that I had never noticed before, and this sent me on a little "rabbit trail." Sure enough, when I got through with my "rabbit trail" I had made an interesting discovery. I had discovered MARY'S FAVORITE PLACE. See if you can find Mary's Favorite Place as you read these three scripture references that mention her name specifically:

1.) Luke 10:38-39 (NAS) – Now as they were traveling along, He [Jesus] entered a certain village; and a woman named Martha welcomed Him into her home. And she had a sister called Mary, who moreover was listening to the Lord's word, seated at His feet.

2.) John 11:32 (NAS) – [At the tomb of Lazarus] Therefore, when Mary came where Jesus was, she saw Him and fell at His feet, saying to Him, "Lord, if You had been here, my brother would not have died."

3.) John 12:3 (NAS) – Mary then took a pound of very costly perfume of pure nard, and anointed the feet of Jesus, and wiped His feet with her hair;

Have you discovered Mary's Favorite Place? Interestingly enough, almost every single time this woman is mentioned in the scriptures she's located in the same place... a place where you and I should visit more frequently.

Matthew 28:8-9 (NAS)
And they left the tomb quickly with fear and great joy and ran to report it to His disciples. And behold, Jesus met them and greeted them. And they came up and took hold of HIS FEET and worshiped Him.

TODAY'S WISDOM NUGGET
If you want to move FORWARD remember these scriptures today:
1. *"Get thee BEHIND me Satan!" Luke 4:8*
2. *"Forgetting those things which are BEHIND, and reaching forth unto those things which are before" Philippians 3:13*
3. *"No man, having put his hand to the plough, and LOOKING BACK, is fit for the kingdom of God" Luke 9:62.*

SEEING THE GOOD
January 3 | July 3

We are living in troubling times. There's not a whole lot of "good" going on around us... at least it appears that way. Psalm 4:6 (A Psalm of David) says, "Many are saying 'Who will show us any GOOD?'" If you're not seeing any GOOD around you, perhaps you're looking in the wrong place.

When you look to this world to find good you will come up empty-handed, much like the people of David's day who said, "Who will show us any good?" You may get glimpses of goodness here and there in this world, but it's a roller coaster ride at best if that's the only place you're looking.

Jesus made it very plain to the rich young ruler when he said, "There is NONE GOOD but one, that is God" (Mark 10:18). So, if you're really wanting to find GOOD you'll need to look to God.

Now, here's where it gets meaty. Jesus said, "Blessed are the pure in heart for they shall see God." So, follow this closely: If you want to see the GOOD you'll have to look to God, and if you want to see GOD you'll need a pure heart. The lack of heart purity is what keeps us from seeing and finding the GOOD because it keeps us from seeing GOD. How do we get pure hearts? David said a prayer like this: "Create in me a clean heart O God, and renew a right spirit within me." (Psalm 51:10)

My Prayer For Today:
"Lord, I want to see the good around me, and when I say that, what I really mean is that I want to see YOU around me. I don't want to be distracted by THE BAD that I see going on. I want to be attracted to THE GOOD that I see in You. Create in me a clean heart, O God, so I can see You and find the Good."

Psalm 24:3-4
Who shall ascend into the hill of the LORD? or who shall stand in his holy place? He that hath clean hands, and a PURE heart....

TODAY'S WISDOM NUGGET
Fear will PARALYZE because fear is a PAIR OF LIES!
Lie #1 "I'm not...I can't...".
Lie #2 "God's not...God can't..."
Refuse to be paralyzed by fear!

WHEN YOU'RE QUIET AND STILL
January 4 | July 4

I woke up early one Fall morning before the sun had risen. I walked down to a wooded area in my neighborhood, found a log and sat down on it, quietly meditating and praying. Because it was chilly that morning, I put on a hoodie and pulled the hood over my head. As I sat there quiet and still a very peculiar thing happened. A robin flew down out of a tree and landed on my head for a brief moment. I suppose in the darkness that my shadowy silhouette looked like a lifeless stump to the bird. Of course I almost jumped out of my skin when I felt the creature land on my head, but after regaining my composure, I was reminded of an important lesson about Nature that morning... when you're quiet and still, things come to you.

Stray dogs and cats don't come up close to people who are moving about... they come to those who are quiet and still. Chipmunks and squirrels tend to be nervous little varmints, but I've had them come up right next to me as I've been quiet and still. I've even had a beautiful red fox come up close to me when I was being extremely quiet and still. THINGS COME TO YOU WHEN YOU'RE QUIET AND STILL.

Most people these days are way too busy. They're looking for some peace and tranquility but it eludes them because they're always in a hurry... always moving... trying to make things happen... always on a schedule and going to the next event. But here's what I've discovered: Peace comes to you when you're quiet and still; ideas come to you when you're quiet and still; inspiration comes to you when you're quiet and still, and most importantly... God comes to you when you're quiet and still.

Psalm 46:10 "Be still and know that I am God."
Isaiah 30:15 (NAS) "In quietness and trust is your strength"
Psalm 131:2 (NIV) "But I have calmed and quieted myself, I am like a weaned child with its mother; like a weaned child I am content."

TODAY'S FOOD FOR THOUGHT
What you believe DEFINES who you are.
What you go through REFINES who you are.
"The trial of your faith, being much more precious than of gold that perisheth, though it be tried with fire, might be found unto praise and honour and glory at the appearing of Jesus Christ" 1 Peter 1:7

DON'T BE SLOPPY!
January 5 | July 5

I ordered a meal at the local Burger King® drive-thru and took it to a near-by park to eat. When I sat down at the picnic table, I searched through the bag to find the napkins. There wasn't a single napkin to be found. Talk about being under pressure! I knew that I couldn't make any kind of mess since there wasn't anything to clean up with. So, I had to eat like a gentle-man instead of a ravenous wolf (like I usually do). I succeeded at not mak-ing a mess and didn't have to wipe my mouth one single time. It's amazing how clean and orderly you can be when there are no options for clean-up.

I guess you could say that napkins give us permission to be sloppy. If I know I have a bag of napkins with me I'm not nearly as concerned about what kind of mess I might make.

These days people use God's mercy like a carry-out bag full of napkins. They anticipate, and even plan on, getting in a mess so they go ahead and ask for a ton of extra napkins. Don't get me wrong. I'm thankful God's mercies are new every morning. I'm thankful when I "mess up" His mer-cy "cleans up," but mercy does not give us permission to live a sloppy life. It just covers us when things do get sloppy. I've heard this saying several dozen times lately: "It's easier to ask for forgiveness than permission." That may be true, but I'm not necessarily trying to do the "easiest" thing. I enjoy a challenge sometimes... like trying to eat a Whopper without having a single napkin on me.

2 Peter 1:5 (NAS)
Now for this very reason also, applying all diligence, in your faith supply MORAL EXCELLENCE...

Romans 6:1-2 (NIV)
What shall we say, then? Shall we go on sinning so that grace may increase? We are those who have died to sin; how can we live in it any longer?

TODAY'S ENCOURAGING WORD

Would you remember Daniel if not for a lion's den? Would you remember David if not for a giant? Would you remember Joshua if not for a wall? If you're facing adversity right now, it's quite possible that you're on the way to a defining moment in your life!

DISTANT
January 6 | July 6

I was reading Jesus' parable of the Prodigal Son when a word "jumped off the page" at me. Jesus said that the prodigal son moved away from his Father's house and "went on a journey into a DISTANT country." (Luke 15:13) There have been times throughout my Christian life when I've said, "God feels so DISTANT from me right now." If you were to be honest about it you would probably admit to having said those very same words. But, as this story so beautifully illustrates, in those times where God feels DISTANT from us it is because we have moved away from Him.

Throughout the story of the Prodigal son, the Father was always found in the same place… IN THE FATHER'S HOUSE. The distance between the son and the Father was created by the son's departure… not the Father. The smartest words that ever left the lips of the Prodigal son are these: "I will arise and go to my Father." He understood that if he wanted to feel close to the Father again that he would need to change locations.

I leave you with these words of admonishment: don't ever accuse God of being DISTANT in your life. Didn't He promise, "I will never leave you nor forsake you?" So, knowing that He is always true to His promises, we must come to the conclusion that when He feels DISTANT from us it is because WE HAVE MOVED.

My Prayer for Today:
"Father, forgive the times that I have wrongly accused You of being DISTANT from me. I realize that the times I've felt that way was due to the waywardness of my own heart. I know the best place for me is in The Father's House… so I will 'dwell in the house of the Lord forever.'"

Hebrews 13:5 (NIV)
God has said, "Never will I leave you; never will I forsake you."

TODAY'S FOOD FOR THOUGHT
Is it just an interesting coincidence that the word DESPAIR is an anagram of the word PRAISED? Perhaps our despair could get turned around if we praised. Think about it!
"Why are you in DESPAIR, O my soul? Hope in God, for I shall again PRAISE Him For the help of His presence." Psalms 42:5 NAS

ASKING QUESTIONS
January 7 | July 7

Asking questions is probably the best way to create engaging conversation. You don't have to look any further than the third chapter of Genesis to discover this point. Did you realize that the first 4 recorded sentences of conversation that God had with man were all questions?

1. Where are you?
2. Who told you that you were naked?
3. Have you eaten from the tree of which I commanded you not to eat?
4. What is this you have done?

Asking questions is a great way of "locating" the person that you are conversing with. By asking questions you can find out what a person is thinking, what they believe in their hearts, and what they have done with their lives.

Some people are blunt and direct in conversation. They make statements and rarely ask questions. To get a person to think about their eternal destiny you could bluntly say, "You're going to hell" or you could ask the question, "Where do you believe you'll spend eternity?" From what I understand about God, I believe He would use the second approach.

In case you think I'm making too big of a deal about this point it might interest you to know that the first recorded words of conversation that Jesus engaged in was also a question… "Why is it that you were looking for me? Did you not know that I had to be in my Father's house?" He spoke these words when he was 12 years old.

Do you think it's just a coincidence that the first recorded conversations of God and Jesus with people were questions? Yes, I'm asking you a question.

Job 38:3 (NLT)
[God speaking to Job] "Brace yourself like a man, because I have some questions for you, and you must answer them."

TODAY'S ENCOURAGING WORD
It's easier to deal with those who are AGAINST YOU
when you realize who is FOR YOU.
*"What then shall we say to these things?
If God is for us, who can be against us?" Romans 8:31 NAS*

NO COASTING!
January 8 | July 8

I was driving up a steep hill one day and, just out of curiosity, I pushed the accelerator all the way to the floor for a moment then took my foot off of the accelerator to see how far the momentum would take me. Surprisingly, I made it to the top of the hill (about 20 yards) simply by coasting uphill with the momentum I had gained. Yes, I suppose you could say that I "coasted uphill."

Coasting uphill, however, is not easily achieved and is rarely done. No, going uphill usually requires the exertion of energy and a large amount of resistance. The downward pull of gravity is a powerful force to be reckoned with, making the idea of "coasting uphill" almost an absurdity.

Going downhill, on the other hand, you can coast all day long without exerting any energy whatsoever. But who wants to go downhill all the time? I like getting to the high places, and if it requires extra energy and a little sweat then so be it. That's why I have adopted this two-word phrase as one of my slogans for life: "No Coasting!" Coasting will almost always take us downhill... a direction that few of us enjoy! So, let's put the pedal to the medal and climb some mountains!

My Confession for Today:
"I reject the easy way, the lazy way, and the 'path of least resistance.' I know that God is calling me to higher places in my life. I know energy will be required, and a certain amount of stamina and fortitude. I will pursue all that God has for me with the strength that He provides. I refuse to coast!"

Philippians 3:14 (NAS) "I press on toward the goal for the prize of the UPWARD call of God in Christ Jesus."

TODAY'S WISDOM NUGGET

Notice the word RESIST in the following verses:
"God resisteth the proud but giveth grace to the humble." James 4:6
"Resist the Devil and he will flee from you." James 4:7.
The same action we are supposed to take against the enemy of our soul is the same action God takes against those who are proud.
Lord, don't RESIST me... help me stay humble!

14

THE DOORWAY TO HEAVEN
January 9 | July 9

I was teaching a congregation the importance of children's ministry one Sunday morning. I wanted to use an illustration that would help the people understand one of Jesus' statements: "Except ye be converted, and become as little children, ye shall not enter into the kingdom of heaven." So, I called two little elementary children to the front of the church and asked them to face each other and form a little "doorway" by raising their hands and putting them together. I then asked several children in the church to come forward and enter the doorway that the two children had created (sort of like playing "London Bridge is Falling Down"). They all walked through the doorway easily with plenty of clearance and room to spare. Then I asked a 6'4" man in the congregation if he would come forward and try to go through the doorway that the two children had created. As you might imagine it was quite an amusing scene as the two children's eyes got big, wondering if their doorway was going to be big enough for the enormous man to enter. The only way the man could pass through the "doorway" was for him to get down on his knees... he had to HUMBLE himself to go through the doorway they had created.

You see, the doorway to the kingdom of Heaven is just the right size for a child to walk through unimpeded, but grown adults have to humble themselves and get on their knees to make it through the passageway. And that's one of the main reasons why many have not yet entered the kingdom of Heaven. Entering the kingdom of Heaven requires humility. A person has to admit that their way of doing things has not worked... that change is necessary... that they can't make it to Heaven on their own. It's best to do this when you're down on your knees, in a very vulnerable state. Yes, it's a humbling event for an adult, but a child can do it easily!

Matthew 19:14 (NIV)
Jesus said, "Let the little children come to me, and do not hinder them, for the kingdom of heaven belongs to such as these."

TODAY'S WISDOM NUGGET
The pendulum on the clock swings far right, then far left... and somewhere in between the two extremes it always hits the exact center. *"Lord, though we all have our extremes, continue to bring us back to the center of what's really important in life."*

WHEN THINGS SEEM MUNDANE
January 10 | July 10

The book of Luke tells us that Jesus was 30 years old on the day he was baptized. The heavens opened, the Holy Spirit descended upon him in the form of a dove, and a voice came from Heaven which said, "This is my beloved Son in whom I am well-pleased." Miraculous! When I read that account I often forget that Jesus, the son of God, went through 30 whole years of his life before any kind of miraculous event took place.

Up until his baptism day, his life was just as ordinary (and possibly mundane) as yours and mine. No extraordinary events that were particularly noteworthy are recorded (besides His birth). He worked in Joseph's carpentry shop... he cleaned his room... he went to the market for His mother... Ho-Hum! But to say that this period of time in his life was unfruitful or unimportant would be a mistake. Everything he did up until he was 30 was as much a part of his purpose on Earth as the 3 years of miracles and teaching that are recorded in the Gospels.

Unfortunately, we live in a society that measures success by milestones and achievements. Just think... by today's standards, Jesus at the age of 29, would have been considered nothing more than just an average Joe... just a carpenter from Nazareth.

When you look at your life you may think, "I don't amount to much... I have achieved little... nothing noteworthy has happened." Do you know Jesus could have said the same thing when He was 29?! But everything changed in one moment in time on the day He was baptized at the age of 30.

Let this serve as encouragement to you. Everything can change in one single moment in time. Even today you just might walk through an unseen door that propels you into your destiny and future... a door that will only be entered because you've proven yourself faithful in the little things... even during the mundane, ordinary days of your life.

TODAY'S WORD OF EXHORTATION
MANY THINGS try to distract us from the ONE THING that is really important. Stay focused on the "ONE THING."
"Martha, Martha," the Lord answered, "you are worried and upset about MANY THINGS, but only ONE THING is needed." Luke 10:41-42 NIV

DEALING WITH IMPERFECTIONS
January 11 | July 11

When I was 15 years old I had a hunger inside of me to learn how to play the guitar. A lady at my church gave me one of her old guitars so I could learn to play. I was appreciative of the gift, but there was one small problem with the guitar... the tuning key for the bottom E string was broken, so that string could not be properly tuned. Did I let that hinder me from learning to play the guitar? No! I just tuned all of the other strings to the one string that couldn't be tightened or loosened. The guitar was "in tune"... just not in "perfect" tune. The hunger to succeed got me past the imperfection I was dealing with.

Ecclesiastes 11:4, in the New Century Version of the Bible, says: "Those who wait for perfect weather will never plant seeds." How true! When Adam and Eve sinned, it threw the whole world into a state of IMPER-FECTION. Nothing here on Earth is perfect... no person, no situation, no organization, no product, no government, etc., etc. We are continually having to deal with imperfections in this life. Nothing, NOT ONE THING, will get done here on earth if you're waiting for things to be perfect first.

The good news is that we're all on a level playing field due to this fact. Everyone who has ever succeeded at anything did it by overcoming an imperfect situation. Sure, there are varying levels of imperfection... some things have fewer imperfections so we call them "EASY," while other things have more imperfections so we call them "DIFFICULT." Still, when all is said and done, an imperfection has to be conquered, one way or the other, in order to get things accomplished.

So, keep on pushing through the imperfections you face, and put your trust in the perfect God who delights in taking imperfect situations and changing them. After all, a "miracle" is just an imperfect situation that has been touched by a perfect God.

TODAY'S FOOD FOR THOUGHT

When I was a little boy, the slide at the playground seemed gigantic to me... but it really wasn't. When I was a teenager, the pimple on my face seemed absolutely enormous... but it really wasn't. Even though I'm much older now, I wonder if there are things that I'm facing that seem to be much bigger than they really are?

TETELESTAI!
January 12 | July 12

"Tetelestai." You may have never heard this Greek word before but I'm sure you know the person who is well-known for saying it. Here is how the word got its origin:

> When the kings of ancient times went to battle and one king defeated another king, he would parade the defeated king before his people in chains as a humiliating public spectacle. After making the defeated king bow before him, he would then place his foot upon the defeated king's head and cry out, "Tetelestai" which translated means: "It has been accomplished!"

You know of someone who used this word from a most unusual place. Jesus cried it out from the cross... Tetelestai!... "It is finished!" In what most people consider to be His weakest moment on Earth, the Prince of Peace was victorious over the Prince of Darkness! Although the serpent had wounded the Savior's heel... the Savior had crushed the serpent's head!

Colossians 2:15 (NIV): And having disarmed the powers and authorities, he made a public spectacle of them, triumphing over them by the cross.

A BRIEF HISTORY OF "WORDS"

In the beginning God used words to create everything. Then God used words to bless everything He had created. Then, Satan used words to deceive man. Then, man used words to blame somebody else for his wrong. Then, God used words to curse the works of man's hands. When God saw both the great joy and sorrow that words caused, He sent His Son, whom He called the WORD (John 1:1) to pay the penalty for man's sin. Now, in order to get right with God, a man must say the words... "Jesus is Lord!" (Romans 10:9). And you thought words weren't that important? My Word!

TODAY'S FOOD FOR THOUGHT

If I have a gift for you in my hand with your name on it, is it yours while it's still in my hand? No. The gift does not become yours until you RECEIVE it (take possession of it). Salvation is a free gift with your name on it. But it doesn't become yours until you RECEIVE it. God has good gifts for His children... but they must be RECEIVED.

DO YOU HAVE "BELIEF" OR "FAITH"?
January 13 | July 13

Are BELIEF and FAITH the same thing? For the longest time I thought they were interchangeable words, having the same meaning. I'm not sure why it's took me so long to understand, but I now know that BELIEF and FAITH are two different things.

You see, you can have a BELIEF that you carry "inside" you your whole life. If you never act on that BELIEF it will not do you any good. For example, you can BELIEVE that a microwave can cook a slice of bacon. You can BELIEVE that your entire life. But, until you stick a slice of bacon in the microwave and push the power button, all you have is a BELIEF (and uncooked bacon). But, when you take a slice of bacon, stick it in the microwave and push the power button, your belief has been activated. You have just experienced the meaning of faith. FAITH has an action attached to it.

BELIEF is inward... FAITH is outward. BELIEF can't be seen in a person... FAITH can.

For the longest time I stumbled over the definition of FAITH as it is recorded in Hebrews 11:1. It says that "Faith is the substance of things hoped for, the evidence of things not seen." All this time I was confused because I thought FAITH and BELIEF were the same thing, but Hebrews is saying FAITH is SUBSTANCE and EVIDENCE. It's tangible. It can be SEEN. It is an unseen BELIEF that has been activated.

A story is told of a tight rope walker who was going to walk a tight rope across Niagara Falls. He asked the surrounding crowd, "Do you BELIEVE I can do this?" All the people shouted, "Yes! We believe!" The tightrope walker then singled out a man in the crowd and asked him, "Do you BELIEVE I can do this?" The man replied, "Yes! I believe!" So the tightrope walker said, "If you BELIEVE I can do it then you come with me. I will carry you on my back!" Suddenly the man's BELIEF was challenged, but eventually, the man agreed to let the tightrope walker carry him across Niagara Falls on his back. His BELIEF was turned into FAITH because the people could SEE his BELIEF in action.

Ephesians 2:8 says, "For by grace you have been saved THROUGH FAITH...." We are not saved simply by BELIEVING in Jesus, but by an action of FAITH. Are your actions in keeping with your inward BELIEFS?

James 2:17 (NIV)
In the same way, faith by itself, if it is not accompanied by action, is dead.

DO NOT GO THERE!
January 14 | July 14

There are three places I've been tempted to go,
Three places where "love, joy and peace" cannot grow.
So, I've got some advice that I'd like to share,
Just 4 simple words... DO NOT GO THERE.

There's a place called WORRY where you wring your hands,
And you fret about things that you don't understand.
When you're in WORRY you negate the power of prayer,
So please take my advice... DO NOT GO THERE!

There's a place called FEAR, and it's cold and dark,
When you pass by FEAR keep driving... don't park!
FEAR is a mirage, it's just a hollow scare,
Again, take my advice... DO NOT GO THERE!

There's a place called ANGER where your blood pressure rises,
Turns molehills into mountains, and inconvenience into crisis.
You'll never have peace when in ANGER, so beware,
Yes, ANGER is a place, so DO NOT GO THERE!

I've been to all three so I know whence I speak.
In these three places the strong become weak.
WORRY, FEAR and ANGER... they're a giant snare,
Please, take my advice... DO NOT GO THERE!

Luke 12:25-26 (NIV)
Who of you by worrying can add a single hour to his lifespan? So if you cannot do such a small thing, why do you worry about the rest?

1 John 4:18 (KJV)
There is no fear in love; but perfect love casteth out fear:

James 1:20 (NAS)
For the anger of man does not achieve the righteousness of God.

TODAY'S WISDOM NUGGET

An enemy will stab you in the back... A friend will stab you in the front.
"Faithful are the WOUNDS of a friend,
But deceitful are the kisses of an enemy." Proverbs 27:6

RESPECT YOUR ELDERS
January 15 | July 15

One summer, while at the beach on vacation, I and my family were playing shuffleboard at the condo where we were staying. We didn't know the rules or score-keeping of the game but we were enjoying it just the same. An older couple walked up and began to watch us play. We asked them if they wanted to join us and they told us that they were supposed to meet another couple there to play so we continued on playing.

About 5 minutes passed by and the couple was still sitting there waiting. They remarked, "Well, it looks like the other couple isn't coming." Upon hearing that we asked them again to join us in our game. It's then that we learned their names (Norman and Elaine) and got to know a little bit about them and their history. Elaine said, "The other couple that said they'd meet us here was a much younger couple... I guess nobody wants to do anything with a couple of old folks." It is then that I stopped asking them to play with us and insisted on it as I handed Elaine one of the shuffleboard cue sticks.

Norman just wanted to sit and watch as Elaine and my wife played against me and my son. Elaine knew all the rules of the game and how to keep score... her years of experience and knowledge of the game ended our ignorance on how to play the game correctly. It turns out that we needed this older couple just as much as they needed us. It was a mutually beneficial relationship that enhanced our vacation at the beach. Thanks Norman and Elaine!

Please remember to be kind to older people... one day you will be one... and most likely others will treat you the way that you treated the elderly when you were younger. It's called "reaping what you sow."

Galatians 6:7
Be not deceived; God is not mocked: for whatsoever a man soweth, that shall he also reap.

TODAY'S WISDOM NUGGET
Not everything that ENTERS your head should EXIT your mouth.
"Fools find no pleasure in understanding but delight in airing their own opinions." Proverbs 18:2 NIV

A SPIRITUAL TOUCH
January 16 | July 16

I was reviewing a previous week's lesson on "The Woman with the Issue of Blood" with my elementary kids at church one Wednesday night. She was miraculously healed simply by touching the hem of Jesus' garment.

I said to the kids, "Lots of people were crowding around Jesus and touching Him that day. What was different about the woman's touch that helped her get healed?" One little boy raised his hand and answered, "It was a spiritual touch!" That was not the answer I was looking for... it was far better than the answer I was looking for. I suppose my jaw dropped to the floor when I heard the little boy's answer. Such profound simplicity. It was one of those "Out of the Mouths of Babes" moments where I became the student instead of the teacher.

There is an emptiness in the spirit of man that longs to be filled. Man's misunderstanding of this emptiness leads him to reach out and touch the physical world to try and fill that void. Today, hundreds of thousands of people will crowd around Jesus desiring to get close enough to touch Him. It's definitely a worth-while endeavor. But, what will be the goal of that touch? Will it only be a physical touch, a touch to satisfy curiosity, an opportunity to "rub elbows with Divinity," or will it be a SPIRITUAL TOUCH, where an inward transaction takes place, unseen by those who only notice "the physical." I'm certain that all of my physical problems and struggles would cease if I could just press through the crowd and touch Jesus... with a SPIRITUAL TOUCH.

Luke 8:45-46
And Jesus said, Who touched me? When all denied, Peter and they that were with him said, Master, the multitude throng thee and press thee, and sayest thou, Who touched me? And Jesus said, Somebody hath touched me: for I perceive that virtue is gone out of me.

TODAY'S WISDOM NUGGET

"I have set before you an OPEN DOOR..." Revelation 3:8
"I will give you the KEYS of the kingdom of heaven..." Matthew 16:19
Some doors you come to in life are wide open... others need a key.
Don't forget the One who holds the keys!

THE EYES OF A CHILD
January 17 | July 17

All who live have one thing in common,
From the lowly simpleton to the wise old shaman.
Both the strong and the weak, the tame and the wild,
We have all seen through the eyes of a child.

Yes, we were all babes, at one time or another,
Each quite dependent on father or mother.
Helplessly needing their care and attention,
The world was brand new without strife or dissension.

In ignorant bliss of life's reality,
We didn't know hatred, had no enemy.
Our knowledge was limited. But, we laughed and we smiled.
What purity and innocence we had as a child.

But now we've grown older, no innocence at all.
Our brains are enlarged, but our hearts are so small.
So easily angered, so quickly offended,
It's so sad to see that our innocence has ended.

So I make this request, yes I have one plea,
That the child once in you sees the child once in me.
And just for a moment let's return to our youth,
Revisit our beginning, remember simple truth.

Go back to a time when our hearts weren't defiled
To the time we all saw through the eyes of a child.

Matthew 18:1-3 (NIV)
At that time the disciples came to Jesus and asked, "Who, then, is the greatest in the kingdom of heaven?" He called a little child to him, and placed the child among them. And he said: "Truly I tell you, unless you change and become like little children, you will never enter the kingdom of heaven."

TODAY'S WISDOM NUGGET
Here's a thought: If God's KINDNESS leads us to repentance (according to Romans 2:4) I wonder if our KINDNESS towards others will lead them to repentance? Is somebody ticking you off? Be kind.

CAN'T FIGHT A FEELING???

January 18 | July 18

I woke up one morning with the most peculiar song stuck in my head. A song from the 1980s called "I Can't Fight This Feeling Anymore" by REO Speedwagon. I have no idea where that song came from, but since I couldn't get it out of my head I started thinking about what the song was saying... that a feeling can be so strong that you can't fight it. Now, according to my understanding of what a "feeling" is, it is nothing more than a thought, or an imagination, with an emotion attached to it. It doesn't have muscles, it doesn't carry a concealed weapon, it hasn't been trained in hand-to-hand combat... the only power it has is what a person gives it. Let's face it, you've got to be pretty weak if you're not able to "fight a feeling."

The enemies we face in life come in varying shapes and sizes. Feelings that steal our joy and peace are one of the smallest enemies that we have to deal with. They can make us sad when we should be happy. They can make us angry when we should be thankful. If we can't learn to "wage war" against them, they will conquer us and make us ineffective in fighting the bigger enemies we face in life. To be overpowered by a feeling is a defeat, and we need to see it that way.

I know, having said this, that I possibly might have hurt your feelings... GOOD. If I've wounded them and hurt them badly enough maybe they'll loose some of their strength and power over you, and maybe next time you get in a battle with them you'll be able to fight them... and CONQUER THEM.

My Prayer for Today:
"Lord, give me victory today over my feelings and emotions that conflict with the truth that I find in Your Word."

2 Corinthians 10:5 "Casting down imaginations, and every high thing that exalteth itself against the knowledge of God, and bringing into captivity every thought to the obedience of Christ."

TODAY'S ENCOURAGING WORD

"In the shadow of His hand He has concealed Me... He has also made Me a select arrow; He has hidden Me in His quiver." Isaiah 49:2 NAS
Make this confession: "I am a secret weapon in God's arsenal. He will pull me out and use me at the proper time."

FIFTY SIX DOLLARS
January 19 | July 19

$56...I remember the exact amount of money that was in my wallet that day... the day I became FREE from the love of money.

It was on a Sunday night at church after a missionary to South America shared his story and an offering was being taken for his ministry. I was a new father, concerned with all of the cares involved in raising a child on a very modest salary. My wife and I had added up all of our weekly expenses and we knew exactly how much money it would take to get through each week. The offering plate was about to come down my row. I opened my wallet and saw that meager amount of money that I would live off of for the next week until my next pay check.... $56. I was trying to decide how much of that money I could conceivably do without in order to give to the offering.

The offering plate was getting closer. My rational thinking was battling against my trust in God. The miser within me was trying to defeat the child of God I longed to be. And then, in a moment, the battle was over as I grabbed the offering plate and emptied my wallet of its contents... the whole $56. In that moment it seemed that a bright light shone, that all of my cares and worries dissipated, that an incomprehensible joy and peace came over me. Why was I so happy? Because I was truly FREE from the bondage to money. It no longer mattered what could be purchased with that $56. It no longer mattered what I would have to "do without" in the upcoming days. I was truly free... just like a slave being released from his shackles. It was then I discovered that it's better to be a broke FREE man than a slave with money in his pocket. The freedom I experienced in that moment was worth millions of dollars, yet, it only cost me.......$56.

Hebrews 13:5 (NIV)
Keep your lives free from the love of money and be content with what you have, because God has said, "Never will I leave you; never will I forsake you."

TODAY'S ENCOURAGING WORD
Try pouring a bucket full of water into a thimble and you will begin to understand the difficulty God faces when He tries to pour His limitless blessing into our limited containers. *"Lord, increase our capacity to receive and contain all that You have for us. Amen."*

AN ETERNAL REMINDER
January 20 | July 20

I have a scar on my right hand. It's been there for over 40 years. It's a constant reminder to me of a windy summer day when I was 8 years old growing up in South Carolina. I had built a fort in my backyard out of boards from a large wooden crate. While I was playing inside the fort a gust of wind blew it over on top of me. As I pushed back the boards and pulled myself out of the wreckage my hand raked across an exposed nail creating a two-inch-long gash that bled profusely. To this day, when I look at that scar I can remember the pain, the blood and the fear of that moment... even though it was over 40 years ago. I'm sure everyone reading this has a similar story about a scar on their body. The pain is gone but the scar remains to remind us of the pain.

Now, in Heaven it is said that there is no crying, pain or sorrow (Revelation 21:4). All of Earth's struggles, defeats, depression and fear are no longer remembered. Humans who inherit this eternal blessing are only aware of constant bliss. Yet, in Heaven there is one single reminder of Earth's pain and sorrow. It is found in the scars upon Jesus' body... in his hands, feet and side. Should a time come in the eternal future, 100,000 years from now, that an individual should ask, "Why is it that Jesus gets all the glory and attention here in Heaven?" the reply will be, "Just look at His scars!"

Those scars are a reminder to us, now and throughout eternity, of the great sacrifice He made for us when He was 33 years old... when He was nailed to a rugged cross... when His blood was spilled for the sins of mankind... when He redeemed you and me. Thank God for the scars of Jesus today... you will continue to see them throughout eternity.

Zechariah 13:6
And one shall say unto him, "What are these wounds in thine hands?" Then he shall answer, "Those with which I was wounded in the house of my friends."

TODAY'S ENCOURAGING WORD
Don't think you have much to offer? Neither did the little boy with a sack lunch of 5 loaves and 2 small fish. God delights in taking people who have very little and feeding multitudes with it. You have more to offer than you think!

FOR MY OWN SAKE
January 21 | July 21

Isaiah 43:25
"I, even I, am the one who wipes out your transgressions for My own sake, And I will not remember your sins." [God speaking]

Why do I forgive people when they do me wrong? I do it for the same reason God does it... FOR MY OWN SAKE. Yes, I know that forgiving is the "right" thing to do. Yes, I know that forgiving releases the offender from having to pay for their sins against me. Yes, I know that I make the world a better place by offering forgiveness to others. But when none of these reasons seem to work, I do it FOR MY OWN SAKE.

Unforgiveness is a darkness within my soul... but I love light, so I will forgive. Unforgiveness is a heaviness and a bondage... but I love freedom, so I will forgive. Unforgiveness creates a sadness in me... but I love to be cheerful, so I will forgive. Unforgiveness is an ugliness within me... but I'm a lover of beauty, so I will forgive. Unforgiveness is a sin... but I am called to be pure and holy, so I will forgive.

Why does God forgive us of our wrongs? Not just for our sake... He does it FOR HIS SAKE. God can't carry unforgiveness because it is sin... and HE CANNOT SIN... HE IS PURE AND HOLY.

Some might say, "If He doesn't hold unforgiveness toward anyone, why does He still send people to Hell?" Fair question. Do you understand, though, that you can offer forgiveness to someone without them receiving it, in the same way you can give a gift to someone without them ever opening the gift. It is not the "gift-givers" fault if the receiver won't accept the gift. The gift-giver did the "right thing" even if the receiver didn't.

God offers us forgiveness, and it would be wise for us to receive it. But, even if we refuse to receive it, God remains forgiving... FOR HIS OWN SAKE.

TODAY'S ENCOURAGING WORD
We all measure success differently. A beginning archer counts it a success just to hit the target with an arrow. An expert archer will be satisfied only if he hits the bullseye. Don't minimize your successes by comparing them with someone else's! (2 Corinthians 10:12)

THE FULLNESS OF TIME
January 22 | July 22

Why was Jesus born the year that he was born? Why wasn't He born 200 years or 500 years earlier (or later for that matter)? And, why didn't He start his ministry at the age of 18 or 25 or 27? Why did it start when He was 30 years old? The answer to these questions is captured in a single verse in Galatians chapter 4, "But when the FULLNESS OF TIME had come, God sent forth his Son…" (Galatians 4:4). There was a set time for Him to be born, a set time for Him to start His ministry and a set time for Him to die. The reason everything happened when it did is because THE FULLNESS OF TIME had come.

There is also a fullness of time for each of us in our lives. That is why it is so important for us to learn patience. Many would like to "speed up" the processes in their lives. Impatience leads us to make decisions out-of-step with God's perfect timing… before the fullness of time has arrived. Those who are too impatient to wait on "the fullness of time" will have to be content with grape juice even though they prefer the taste of wine. Wine can only be made after the fullness of time has been observed.

If you're disappointed that things aren't happening for you in the time frame you had hoped may I suggest that maybe God's "set time" for you has not yet come… that the fullness of time has yet to be reached… that exhibiting patience is the very best thing that you can do in this present moment. Patience says, "God, I trust You, that You will get everything to me in the proper time. I can wait until the fullness of time has come for me." If you understand and believe that God has perfect timing it releases you from worry, impatience and fear about the future.

He's in control and He has perfect timing. You can count on that… every time!

Ecclesiastes 3:11 (NIV) "He has made everything beautiful in its time."

TODAY'S ENCOURAGING WORD
A pearl is just an irritation that's been covered with beauty. God can take your irritants and ashes and turn them into something beautiful! *"To appoint unto them that mourn in Zion, to give unto them BEAUTY for ASHES, the oil of joy for mourning, the garment of praise for the spirit of heaviness." Isaiah 61:3*

HARD AND COLD
January 23 | July 23

A stick of butter was sitting out on the counter in our kitchen. I asked my wife, "Did you leave this out on purpose?" She replied, "Yes, I'm sitting it out so it can soften." The wheels started turning in my head, almost like I've never understood the cause and effect relationships associated with heat and cold. I guess you'd call it "revelation" even though it's all quite elementary. You see, the colder a thing gets the harder it gets. Science tells us that when something gets cold, all of the molecules that compose it bond closer together. When something is heated the molecules pull away from each other and the thing softens. This is true of almost all the major elements on earth, from water to gold…. and, yes, even butter.

This draws me to my thought for today. Why are there so many hard people with hardened hearts all around? It's simple… THEY ARE COLD. Jesus said, "Because lawlessness is increased, most people's love will grow cold" (Matthew 24:12). When love grows cold hearts get hard… it's just a fact of nature. So, the question is, "Can a hard heart be softened again?" The answer is a definite "YES"……. But, heat will need to be applied.

My Prayer For Today:
"Lord, I don't want my heart to grow cold. I see the shape the world is in, and I'm grieved by the way people act, but I know I can't let that "get" to me if I'm going to live a life that's pleasing to you. I refuse to be hard and cold. But it will take more than just grit and determination to avoid getting cold… it will take the indwelling presence of Your Holy Spirit. As He burns within my heart I know there's no way I can grow cold. Holy Spirit, BURN IN ME!"

Luke 3:16
John answered, saying unto them all, I indeed baptize you with water; but one mightier than I cometh, the latchet of whose shoes I am not worthy to unloose: he shall baptize you with the Holy Ghost and with FIRE.

TODAY'S ENCOURAGING WORD
POTENT: Having great power. POTENTIAL: Having great possibility. God is potent. In fact, He's called Omnipotent which means "all powerful." If the Potent One is in you then it only stands to reason that you must have great POTENTIAL.
Greater is He that is in you, than he that is in the world! 1 John 4:4

WHEN A SLAVE BECOMES KING
January 24 | July 24

Why did it take the children of Israel 40 years to enter into the Promised Land? I've heard many good explanations, and would like to add just one more for consideration. Proverbs 30:21-22 tells us, "Under three things the earth quakes, And under four, it cannot bear up: Under a slave when he becomes king...."

The Israelites had lived as slaves in Egypt for 400 years. It's the only lifestyle they knew. God was taking them to a land where they would no longer be slaves. They would be conquerors, and very much like "kings" in the land He was taking them to. But Proverbs tells us that the "earth quakes" under a slave when he becomes king. So what needed to happen was the "slave mentality" had to be rooted out of the Israelites. How do we know the Israelites had a "slave mentality?" Because, when things were getting tough in the wilderness there was a large group of Israelites who wanted to return to Egypt so they could eat the "leeks, onions, and garlic" that they once ate as slaves. (Numbers 11:5) Yet, God had told them that the Promised Land was a land flowing with "Milk and Honey." If you prefer leeks, onions and garlic over milk and honey you're showing that you're content in being a slave (and you probably also have really bad breath!).

All of that was under the Old Covenant. Today, we are under a New Covenant, and God has a Promised Land for us as well. It's a land flowing with "milk and honey" where He wants us to reign as kings. 1 Peter 2:9 tells us that we are a "chosen generation, a ROYAL priesthood...." ROYAL! We are supposed to reign like kings in this life. But if we have a slave mentality, where we prefer bondage to man's ways, where we prefer government assistance over Heavenly provision, the "earth quakes" in our presence. Child of God, you're royalty! Don't act like a slave... it messes up Earth's balance. Could it be that many are going through a "wilderness" in their lives simply because they have a slave mentality instead of royal one?

Revelation 5:10
And hast made us unto our God kings and priests: and we shall reign on the earth.

TODAY'S ENCOURAGING WORD
If you don't like the season you're in, hang in there... seasons change.

REVELATION FROM A STAIN
January 25 | July 25

The year was 1987. I was at my home church, Trinity Chapel, on Sunday morning and we were observing Communion. The Communion trays were being handed out as I sat on the pew next to my friend Ronnie Crites. It was a somber and solemn moment as we reflected on the death of our Savior and the blood that he spilled for us as a sacrifice. Soft worship music was being played. The juice tray was handed to me and I took out my cup as I handed the tray to Ronnie. He grabbed his cup and then grabbed the tray. Somehow during the exchange of hands Ronnie accidentally spilled his cup of grape juice on me. The stain quickly sank in to my khaki pants. For just a second there was complete silence as we both looked down at the spreading stain. Ronnie's eyes got big as he looked up at me as if to say, "Oh man, I'm so sorry!" Then I looked at him and said, "That's the blood of Jesus spilled for you and me!" And then it happened… that wonderful revelation of what Jesus did when he spilled his blood became REAL to us, and in a split second we both started crying… no, crying is not the right word… we sobbed! The reality of what Christ did for us was made plain as we looked at that stain on my pants… that awful, ugly, BEAUTIFUL stain.

The stain on my pants was just an accident… the stain on the cross was very much on purpose. The stain on my pants was a minor inconvenience… the stain on the cross cost Jesus His life. The stain on my pants was temporary and would soon be washed away… the stain on the cross was permanent and will never lose its power to wash away the sins of even the vilest sinner. "What can wash away my sins? Nothing but the blood of Jesus!" Yes, the spill and the resulting stain that appeared that Sunday morning was an accident… a wonderful, revelation-filled accident that I will forever remember… then again, maybe it wasn't an accident at all.

1 Peter 1:18-19
Forasmuch as ye know that ye were not redeemed with corruptible things, as silver and gold,… But with the precious blood of Christ, as of a lamb without blemish and without spot"

TODAY'S FOOD FOR THOUGHT
"He sent his word, and healed them…" Psalm 107:20. God sends His word to heal people… what do you send your words to do?

LEARN FROM THE APPLE TREE
January 26 | July 26

One day, you will wake up and realize that all the things you once looked FORWARD to when you were younger are now BEHIND you. You will be tempted to look BACKWARDS in time to find happiness and joy... remembering the good ol' days when you were younger and your "life" was ahead of you. Don't give in to those thoughts!

Do you think that the giant apple tree benefits at all from remembering when it was a young sapling? When it was a sapling it had no height, no depth of root, no fruit on its branches. It struggled through the changing of the seasons, the cold of winter, and the blights and parasites that attack young trees. It fought to stay alive through times of drought and harsh conditions. Its goal was to become a fruit-bearer... to have depth of root... to grow tall and stout. When this is finally achieved would it not be nonsense to wish for its younger years back? Now it is tall, mature, strong, and bearing fruit. It has something to offer the world. You do too!

You are now seasoned, experienced, wise and discerning. You have something to offer the world now. All of your energy is not focused upon yourself. You can meet the needs of others. Others can benefit from your experiences and years of wisdom. Nephews, nieces and grandchildren can climb up into your arms (your branches) because you are mature, strong and stable. Others can come to you for wisdom and advice knowing that you have stood the test of time and your roots have dug deep into the earth. You have not been uprooted even though you've gone through many storms. Some will seek fruit from your branches for refreshment and nourishment... love, joy, peace... fruit that is only found on mature trees.

Your best years are not behind you. You are now in your best years... the years that all the seasons of growth have prepared you for. You are now a FRUIT-BEARER.

Psalm 1:3
...he shall be like a tree planted by the rivers of water, that bringeth forth his fruit in his season;... and whatsoever he doeth shall prosper.

TODAY'S WISDOM NUGGET
"Don't always be asking, "Where are the good old days?" Wise folks don't ask questions like that." Ecclesiastes 7:10 (Message Bible)

I AM A BELIEVER
January 27 | July 27

I am a BELIEVER. I carry that name with reverence and humility.

Yes, I am called BELIEVER… not FEELER, for I am led by what I believe and not what I feel. Many times my feelings take a back seat to the things I believe. Emotions can be wonderful… they can manufacture feelings of euphoria and deep satisfaction, but they can also create feelings of hopelessness and depression. I will not be led by them... because I am a BELIEVER.

I am called BELIEVER… not UNDERSTANDER, for I believe many things that I do not fully comprehend with my mind. Believing is an action of the heart and spirit and not one of the mind and brain. It is sometimes seemingly irrational and illogical to my understanding, but it is what I do… because I am a BELIEVER.

I am called BELIEVER… not SEER, for I do not have to see with my eyes what I say I believe in my heart. I believe a story that has been passed down by word of mouth and by the written word from generations past. I am thousands of years removed from the events and people that have created faith in me. I do not have video footage or photographs lending visible proof to the things I believe in. Yet, I still trust and hold on tightly to stories and teachings that have changed my life and the lives of so many others… because I am a BELIEVER.

Gone forever are the days when I was called DOUBTER, SKEPTIC and UNBELIEVER. Others may mock me because of my child-like faith in an invisible God whose love I confess to have experienced. Many do not understand why I am so passionate about an unseen kingdom and about truths that I believe must be accepted and adhered to in order to find true peace and happiness in life. I might even make some people uncomfortable by making my confession and claims of faith, but I cannot apologize. I have come too far to shrink back from this life of faith… it is my cornerstone and foundation… it is who I am… I AM A BELIEVER.

John 3:16 (NIV)
…whoever BELIEVES in him shall not perish but have eternal life.

TODAY'S WISDOM NUGGET
In the Christian Life: Love is the EVIDENCE, Faith is the CONFIDENCE, And Joy is the CONSEQUENCE. (John 15:11)

METAMORPHOO
January 28 | July 28

Metamorphoo... it's the Greek word for TRANSFORM. You probably recognize it from your days in Science class as you studied the "metamorphosis" of the caterpillar into a butterfly. It is the same word used to describe what happened to Jesus on the Mount of Transfiguration when his appearance changed from that of a normal man to a glistening, shining embodiment of the glory of God... a transformation that three of His disciples witnessed. It is also the same word used in 2 Corinthians 3:18 which states that we (believers) are being "transformed" into the glory of the Lord.

So, let's put all of this together. A caterpillar is nothing more than a butterfly who has not yet manifested its full glory yet. As Jesus walked this earth He contained all of the glory of Heaven everywhere He went but it was "secretly tucked away" and only seen by His three disciples on the Mount of Transfiguration for a short moment in time.

Likewise, the believer has a "hidden glory"... an inward radiance that is concealed from the world's view. If we were to see the glory that is within each other surely our view and opinions of each other would change, even as I'm sure those three disciples looked at Jesus totally different the rest of their days after that encounter on the Mount. Oh, that we could have a "Mount of Transfiguration" experience with the people in our lives so we could see the true glory that is within each one... to see the Heavenly being that is within instead of the fallible, imperfect shell that we often judge one another by. Yes, we're all undergoing change... awaiting the day when the metamorphosis will be complete and the full glory is manifested. But just for today, try to imagine that secret, hidden glory concealed within the people you come into contact with. Perhaps a deeper appreciation for who they REALLY are might result.

2 Corinthians 3:18 (NAS)
But we all, with unveiled face, beholding as in a mirror the glory of the Lord, are being TRANSFORMED into the same image from glory to glory, just as from the Lord, the Spirit.

TODAY'S WISDOM NUGGET
Most people can tell what kind of relationship you have with the INVISIBLE God by the way you treat VISIBLE people. (1 John 4:20)

FINDING GOD'S HEART
January 29 | July 29

Just for a moment, let's not talk about all the things that God permits or the things He overlooks about us because of His great love for us. Let's not talk about how far away from His original plan we can deviate and still remain within the boundaries of His love and mercy. People always want to know where the boundaries and the borders are. But just for a moment lets talk about getting as far from the borders and boundaries as possible… let's talk about finding the core… the center of God's heart.

People want to know, "Does God love gay people, does God love adulterers, does God love thieves, does God love pedophiles, etc.?" The answer is unquestionably YES! He loves all of humanity, so much so that He gave His only Son to die for all of us to eradicate our sins. Let that be forever settled in our minds. BUT, another question needs to be asked: "What is God looking for in a man or woman?" After all, the scripture says that the eyes of Lord search "throughout the earth that He may strongly support those whose heart is completely His." (2 Chronicles 16:9) Are we really only interested in knowing if God loves us? Don't we also want to know that God is STRONGLY SUPPORTING us… that His eyes keep landing on us as He searches the Earth to find someone whose heart is completely HIS?

This is not about "living on the border of God's Love." It's about finding His heart, and moving as close to it as possible. It's about being pleasing to Him. Yes, it is settled. God loves all humanity with great compassion and mercy, but are men seeking to please Him and discover His Heart and His Truths? Or, do they just want to know where the boundary lines are so they can get as far away from His heart as possible and still say that they REMAIN IN HIS LOVE?

Jeremiah 29:13 (NIV)
You will seek me and find me when you seek me with all your heart.

TODAY'S WISDOM NUGGET

QUALIFY, GRATIFY, UNIFY, EDIFY, FORTIFY, and GLORIFY. All these words end with the "IF I" sound. I must never take for granted the part that "I" play in making things work out. "IF I" will apply myself to what needs to be done… "IF I" will give God room to work in my life… "IF I" I will stop making excuses… "IF I" will follow God's instructions found in His word, success will surely come to me.

TWO KINDS OF LIFE
January 30 | July 30

1. ETERNAL LIFE: Life that is fully and completely enjoyed in HEAVEN as a result of receiving salvation through Jesus Christ.

2. ABUNDANT LIFE: Life that is fully and completely enjoyed on EARTH as a result of receiving salvation through Jesus Christ.

Jesus came to give us BOTH of these... something for the "here and now" and something for the "hereafter." We don't have to choose between one or the other... they are both offered. But, it seems that many are only interested in whether or not they have ETERNAL life. Many forfeit their rights to ABUNDANT life on earth because they want to live their own way, instead of living the way prescribed in God's Word. ABUNDANT life brings longevity, fruitfulness and a measure of earthly reward. When you forfeit ABUNDANT life, ETERNAL life usually comes a lot sooner than anticipated.

Many want to know "Can I have ETERNAL life and still maintain a sinful lifestyle?" I'm not going to answer that question. But I will tell you this for sure... You can't have ABUNDANT life and still maintain a sinful lifestyle. The two are in conflict. Abundant life comes from knowing the TRUTH and following it. Jesus said, "The truth will set you free." Freedom is the very first benefit of ABUNDANT living. No one who is completely bound and tethered to a sinful lifestyle can enjoy ABUNDANT life because they don't have freedom. Maybe they will enjoy ETERNAL life... I can't say. But, it seems like if Jesus died to bring us ETERNAL life and ABUNDANT life that we would choose to receive both.

Titus 1:2
In hope of eternal life, which God, that cannot lie, promised before the world began;

John 10:10
I am come that they might have life, and that they might have it more abundantly.

TODAY'S WISDOM NUGGET
REMEMBER: No matter how "right" you may be in your assessment of a situation, a negative and critical attitude will make you look "wrong."

PRAISE... OR REBUKE?
January 31 | July 31

A few years ago I was coaching my son's co-ed soccer team when one of the girls on the team scored her first (and only) goal of the year. I was celebrating on the sidelines, jumping up and down, screaming out her name in victory. In a team huddle after the game I made a really big deal about this girl scoring in the game and continued to pour accolades on her. But she stopped me and said, "The way you're going on and on about it makes it sound like you're surprised that I could even score a goal... like you didn't think I was capable of scoring." Wow. I hadn't thought about it like that so I apologized to her.

When Peter was walking on the water and sank because he took his eyes off of Jesus, Jesus grabbed him, pulled him out of the water and gave him a firm rebuke, saying to him, "Why did you doubt, o ye of little faith!" Jesus DID NOT congratulate Peter for walking on the water (something no other human has done, neither before nor since). Nor, did He hold him up as a shining example of miraculous faith. No, instead He gave him a sharp rebuke. But that rebuke said something to Peter. It said, "I believed you could do it... and you did do it, but you didn't follow through... I expected more from you... you can do better than that, I know you're capable of more!" I realize that's not written in the scripture. It's just a little something extra that I added... a little bit of revelation I got from a young female soccer player.

I'd rather get a firm rebuke from Jesus for not measuring up to what He thinks I'm capable of than to get praise and celebration from people who have little or no expectation out of me whatsoever. What about you?

Matthew 14:30-31 (NIV)
But when he saw the wind, he was afraid and, beginning to sink, cried out, "Lord, save me!" Immediately Jesus reached out his hand and caught him. "You of little faith," he said, "why did you doubt?"

TODAY'S WISDOM NUGGET
One thing the Garden of Eden shows us is that someone can have a perfectly good situation, but not even realize it because they believe the lie that the deceiver told them more than God's Word.
"I have learned in whatever state I am, to be content." Philippians 4:1

HEAVEN AND HELL
February 1 | August 1

While I was speaking on the topic of Eternity at a Bible Study for recovering drug addicts one young man had two interesting (and slightly off-the-wall) observations. Speaking about Hell, he said, "What if there are people who really like pain and torture... Hell wouldn't seem so bad to them and they might actually like it." Speaking of Heaven, he said, "I don't want to live for eternity, that seems like it would get kind of boring after a while."

I let him speak his mind and then replied, "How old are you?" He said "24." I continued, "You are trying to make comparisons of an eternal Heaven and Hell based on your 24 years of experience on Earth. You put your hand on a hot stove and get burned and you think 'I now know what pain is.' You have a really good day filled with smiles, laughter and pleasure on Earth and you think 'I now know what goodness and happiness is.' But I'm telling you that your experiences on Earth, both good and bad, aren't comparable to the agony of an eternal Hell or the bliss of an eternal Heaven. You see beauty and ugliness on Earth and you can tell the difference between the two. But nothing on Earth can prepare you for the striking difference between the true beauty of Heaven and the ugly reality of Hell."

Many are just like this young man... comparing eternal things to temporary, earthly things, thinking they fully understand the ramifications of the decision they make in either serving Christ or rejecting Him. I'm sure that the most rank sinner has no idea of the terrible pain and agony awaiting him in Hell if he does not repent. I'm also pretty sure that the most holy saint hasn't gotten the smallest glimpse of the splendor that awaits him in Heaven.

1 Corinthians 2:9
"Eye hath not seen, nor ear heard, neither have entered into the heart of man, the things which God hath prepared for them that love him."

TODAY'S FOOD FOR THOUGHT
Hurt people are sort of like onions... they usually have a lot of layers to them, and, if you take the time to cut to the core of who they are it will probably bring you to tears.

BLIND BARTIMAEUS... SEEING BARTIMAEUS
February 2 | August 2

Do you realize just how close the story of Blind Bartimaeus came to not appearing in the Bible? As the story goes, Jesus was passing through Bartimaeus' hometown and a multitude of people gathered around Him. Bartimaeus heard that Jesus was passing by so he repeatedly hollered to get His attention, "Jesus, Son of David, have mercy on me!" Evidently, this got on people's nerves and many in the crowd told him to "shut up". But the scriptures tell us that this didn't hinder him. He yelled even louder, until he finally got Jesus' attention, and Jesus called for him to come and stand before Him. The rest of the story? Bartimaeus received his sight… Jesus healed him!

Now, there was a moment in time where this whole story could have totally changed. Had Bartimaeus listened to the crowd when he was told to "shut up"… if he had held his peace… if his concern for what others thought about him had been his motivation that day, his story would have never appeared in the Bible. He would have kept quiet. Jesus would have walked right on by him. The miracle would have never happened. He would have pleased the crowd by "shutting up" and would have gone to his grave as "BLIND Bartimaeus."

Many times in life we come to a cross roads. We come to a place where we must choose to either please the crowd or pursue the Lord, no matter what the cost. Others may get annoyed with us. They won't understand why we are pursuing Jesus with such fervency. They won't understand how desperate we are to capture His attention to have an audience with Him. We will be asked to keep quiet and to calm down. A choice will be made to either keep our peace and please the multitude, or to throw all caution to the wind in full pursuit of the miracle we need from the Lord.

Do you need something that only the Lord can give? If you do, you will definitely need to overcome timidity, the fear of man, and the desire to be a people-pleaser. Just ask "SEEING Bartimaeus."

Mark 10:48 (NET Bible)
Many scolded him to get him to be quiet, but he shouted all the more

TODAY'S WISDOM NUGGET
Peacemakers find similarities… Troublemakers find differences.

DADDY'S CHAIR
February 3 | August 3

When I was a kid growing up in the Lane household the five of us kids could sit at any chair at the supper table we wanted to… any chair, that is, except for the chair at the head of the table. That was my Father's chair. It was just understood. He was the head of the house, the law-maker and the bread-winner, so that honor (and responsibility) gave him the right to sit there… not anyone else.

When I came into God's family I found a similar situation existed. He gives all of His children an opportunity to sit around His table and enjoy the supply and provision that He brings. We can sit at any chair around His table that we like… any chair, that is, except for "Father's Chair." That chair is reserved for Him alone.

It has been called "The Great White Throne" and also "The Judgment Seat." God alone sits in that seat. He alone is qualified to sit there because He knows all and sees all. He alone is KING. He alone is JUDGE. That's the reason He tells us, "Judge Not." When we judge others we are sitting in His seat… and that's the only seat "in the house" that is off-limits. Remember that the next time you are tempted to judge someone.

Here are some of the words to a little song I wrote when I was 19 called "Daddy's Chair":

> He gives us a place at His table
> And He gives us a mansion, too.
> And He lets us walk on streets of gold
> Down "Glory Avenue."
> And all that He has is ours to share
> Just don't go sitting in Daddy's chair.

Revelation 20:11
And I saw a great white throne, and him that sat on it, from whose face the earth and the heaven fled away; and there was found no place for them.

TODAY'S FOOD FOR THOUGHT
I believe that if you treat others badly it will come back to you, either in this life or the next… and if you're lucky it will just be in this one.
"Whatever a man sows, this he will also reap." Galatians 6:7

THE "WORD" BECAME FLESH
February 4 | August 4

I am a very big believer in the POWER OF WORDS. Having said that, however, I'd like to offer the following observation. When God wanted to create the Earth and the Universe it was a simple process... He spoke WORDS... and whatever He spoke came into existence. He showed us the power that words have when He did that. God's WORDS have creative power. (Ours do, too.) BUT, when God wanted to show His love and forgiveness toward mankind it was not as simple as "speaking WORDS." If He could create the Earth and the Universe by speaking words, why could He not extend forgiveness and love to mankind through speaking words? He could have spoken from Heaven, for all to hear, "I love you... You are all forgiven!" But, that was not the solution.

The action of love and forgiveness took something special. John 1:14 tells us that "THE WORD BECAME FLESH and dwelt among us." The answer to the situation did not come by God "speaking WORDS" but rather by God "showing WORDS." The words "I LOVE YOU" and "I FORGIVE YOU" were wrapped in flesh, in the form of Jesus Christ. The spoken words "I love you" can be doubted... but when you see what Christ did when He died on the cross for you and me, you not only HEAR "I love you" you can also SEE "I love you."

You've heard the saying "Actions speak louder than words." Actions are WORDS THAT BECOME FLESH. You can say, "I'm going to go on a diet," but those are just "words" until you follow through with the action... until the WORDS BECOME FLESH. And, you can say, "I love God and give Him my life" but those are just "words" until you follow through with the action... until the WORDS BECOME FLESH.

Yes, words are powerful, but the most powerful words you will speak today may not actually come from your mouth. The most powerful words you speak today will be your WORDS THAT BECOME FLESH AND DWELL AMONG US.

John 1:14 - And the Word was made flesh, and dwelt among us

TODAY'S FOOD FOR THOUGHT
FRIEND: *n. A person with whom one is allied in a struggle or cause.*
You don't really know who your true friends are until you go through a struggle and see who remains allied with you through it.

HE MAKES ME LIE DOWN
February 5 | August 5

I'm amazed by the amount of insomnia (sleeplessness) that people experience these days. Every other commercial on TV advertises some new sleeping aid that's out on the market. One of the most quoted scriptures in the world (Psalm 23) actually has an answer to this dilemma. Just one verse after "The Lord is my shepherd…" we read, "He makes me lie down."

Perhaps you didn't know this, but sheep are very skittish animals. When you see a sheep "lying down" you know that sheep has a GOOD SHEPHERD. There are 3 things in particular that must take place before sheep will LIE DOWN.

1. They must know that there are no predators nearby.
2. They must be free from all irritating pests.
3. They must be completely free from hunger.

If any one of these elements is missing from the equation a sheep will not LIE DOWN. The same holds true for us "skittish humans." That is why Psalm 23 is so meaningful to us… we are just like sheep.

1. For us to be able to go to sleep we must know that our enemy can't harm us. Good News! Jesus defeated our enemy when he cried out from the cross, "It is finished!" No need to lie awake in fear at night! *"In peace I will lie down and sleep, for you alone, O LORD, will keep me safe." Psalm 4:8*

2. All pestering thoughts must be removed. Worry is a huge sleep stealer. Jesus takes our worries away from us so we can experience REST. He is the one who said, *"I am meek and lowly of heart and you will find rest unto your souls." Matthew 11:29*

3. Finally, for us to find rest and sleep we must know that our needs are met. After all, it's hard to sleep when you've got a growling stomach or when bills are stacked to the ceiling. Once again we find a promise in Gods word that He will *"supply all our needs according to His riches in glory by Christ Jesus." Philippians 4:19*

If you've experienced difficulty getting to sleep at night, stop counting sheep… and just be one! The Good Shepherd will bring you rest.

TODAY'S WORD OF ENCOURAGEMENT
To the prayer warriors: What you do in secret is more important than what most other people do in public. *"Then your Father, who sees what is done in secret, will reward you." Matthew 6:6*

BORN THIS WAY?
February 6 | August 6

Some folks think that when they say, "I was born this way" that it is the same as saying, "God made me this way". But that is not the case, and I hope to clear up the confusion on this by sharing a simple little story from the Bible. In John 9 Jesus met a beggar man who was blind. He did something very unusual when he met this man. He spit on the ground, made clay of the spittle and put the clay on the blind man's eyes. He then told the man to go to the pool of Siloam and to wash the clay off of his eyes. When the man did as Jesus said, he received his sight. Now, this was no ordinary blind man, for John 9:1 tells us that he was "blind from birth." He didn't lose his sight through an accident or illness. He was BORN THIS WAY. But, we cannot say, "God made him this way", for if God made him that way then Jesus completely "undid" what God had done when He healed the man. And Jesus is the One who told us "a house divided against itself cannot stand." So for him to "undo" what God "did" would be counter-productive and literally be a HOUSE DIVIDED. The point is, just because the blind man was "born that way" it was not the way Jesus wanted him to stay.

Now, each of us was born with defective DNA. God didn't make us this way... our great grandfather Adam did this to us. Because of his original sin he has passed down defective DNA to all of his descendants. We ALL have the effects of sin that manifest in our lives because of this corrupt DNA. Some have it appear in their physical bodies through abnormalities and disease (like the blind man in the story). Others have it appear in their mind in the form of mental illness and emotional problems. Others have it appear in the form of damaging sinful habits that eventually take their toll on both body and soul. (P.S. In 2004 scientists discovered a gene that causes alcoholism) NO ONE is exempt from the effects of this corrupt DNA... WE WERE BORN THIS WAY. But the good news is: even though we were BORN this way we don't have to stay this way... we can be BORN again!

John 3:7 (NAS)
Do not be amazed that I said to you, 'You must be born again.'

TODAY'S FOOD FOR THOUGHT
To be born once is nice. But it's much better to be born twice!

FEAR IS A LIAR!
February 7 | August 7

I was awakened from sleep one night by the shrill sound of a woman's screams... or at least so I thought. My heart was racing as I immediately raised up out of bed, responding with a fearful panic to the sound I had heard. Fear-filled thoughts entered my mind as I sat on the edge of my bed and listened again to hear where the scream was coming from. But I heard nothing... not another sound. The fear subsided, and my heart got back to a regular rhythm.

Being assured in my mind that all was okay, I laid my head back on my pillow wondering what the sound might have been. I was just about to doze back off to sleep, and that's when I heard it again... it was clear and distinct... it was an irritating "nose whistle" (you know, one of those "whistles" that develops in your nasal cavity that lets off a high pitched whistling sound as you breathe). And to think, fear had "told me" that someone was screaming because something terrible was happening... and I believed it, to the point that my heart was pounding out of my chest, all because of a tiny obstruction in my nose! Now that's sad (but somewhat funny).

It's important to remember this about fear: it will take something relatively small and insignificant and blow it totally out of proportion. It will tell you that the "cold bug" you have is really pneumonia. It will tell you that the pimple on your neck is a malignant tumor. It will tell you that your lack of funds to pay your utility bill this month is the onset of bankruptcy. It will tell you that forgetting where you put your keys is the first stage of dementia. Yes, it will even tell you that the irritating whistle in your nose is the fearful sound of a woman's scream. Don't entertain fear for a second... it's a liar!

Isaiah 41:10 - Fear thou not; for I am with thee: be not dismayed; for I am thy God: I will strengthen thee; yea, I will help thee; yea, I will uphold thee with the right hand of my righteousness.

TODAY'S FOOD FOR THOUGHT
My favorite song title of all time is by a duo from the 80s named Salmond and Muldner. The song title was *"Stumbling Heavenward."* No matter where you are in your "journey" just remember: if you trip and fall, at least make sure that you're falling in the right direction.

44

FEAR AND SIZE RELATIONSHIPS
February 8 | August 8

With my working gloves on, I was moving around some large rocks from my side yard to a backyard fountain that I was building. I picked up one rock and there beneath it sat a creepy black widow spider. Without hesitation, I reached down and smashed it with my finger... a little black pile of goop was all that remained of the deadly spider. For a moment I thought about how fearful most people are of this particular spider and recalled a few horror stories I've heard of people who almost died from its bite. Kind of ironic that such a feared, deadly creature can have its life extinguished so quickly just by smashing it with a finger tip.

FEAR RARELY CONSIDERS SIZE RELATIONSHIPS. A 5 foot tall woman doesn't think twice about jumping up on a chair to get away from a 2 inch tall mouse. That's because fear is not rational, and that is why it is one of the greatest tools of the devil to rob a person of their dignity and their faith.

Generally speaking, this is my rationale concerning fear: If "it" is smaller than me, I can defeat it. If "it" is bigger than me, it's still smaller than God, and God is in me according to 1 John 4:4, so I can defeat it. And, if I can defeat it there is no reason to fear it. Now, that may sound like an arrogant statement to some, but it is only meant as a statement of "confidence and faith," and that is exactly what a person must have to overcome fear.

Here are a couple of good verses to remember when facing fear:

Luke 10:19
Behold, I give unto you power to tread on serpents and scorpions, and over all the power of the enemy: and NOTHING shall by any means hurt you.

Psalm 27:1
The LORD is my light and my salvation; whom shall I fear? the LORD is the strength of my life; of whom shall I be afraid?

TODAY'S WISDOM NUGGET

I used to pray for ME a lot. But then I got this revelation when I was studying The Lord's Prayer. Jesus told us to pray for US:
Give US this day... forgive US or debts... lead US not... deliver US.
My prayer life is different now... I pray for US!

FIGHTING BEELZZZZEBUB!

February 9 | August 9

I was on my regular morning walk on a warm summer day. I stopped at a park bench to sit down for a moment of prayer and to collect my thoughts for the day. Within seconds I found myself under attack from a pesky, irritating, biting fly. I swatted and dodged as the fly harassed me constantly without letting up. When I couldn't stand it any longer I surrendered my place on the bench to get away from the annoying pest.

As I was walking away, though, the word "Beelzebub" popped up in my mind. I remembered that the name "Beelzebub" (a Bible name for Satan) means "Lord of the Flies." Realizing that I had just conceded victory to a stupid fly, I headed back to the park bench to regain my territory.

When I sat down the attacks resumed and I sat there swatting at my enemy, slapping my head and back and waving my arms around like a crazed maniac. I'm sure if anyone had seen me that morning they would have suspected I had some type of mental disorder. But it didn't matter to me what I looked like or what anyone might have thought. I was not going to be beaten by a pesky fly. I stood my ground on that park bench, determined not to surrender this time. After landing quite a few punches I eventually wore the fly down. After several minutes of hand-to-wing combat I overcame my enemy and I saw him buzz off in defeat. Victory had been accomplished. The prayer bench had been reclaimed!

Don't concede small victories to the enemy of your soul. Stand your ground and fight. Small victories lead to bigger ones!

Ephesians 6:10
Finally, my brethren, be strong in the Lord, and in the power of his might.

1 Timothy 6:12
Fight the good fight of faith.

TODAY'S FOOD FOR THOUGHT

2 important facts about breath: 1.) God spoke the animals into existence but when He made Adam He breathed His very own breath into him. 2.) All of your speaking is done when you exhale. CONCLUSION: God gave me my inhale... I wil give Him my exhale. *"Let every thing that hath breath praise the LORD." Psalms 150:6*

NEED STRENGTH? SEEK HIS PRESENCE
February 10 | August 10

This morning a simple prayer was in my heart so I prayed it out loud, "Lord, give me strength." As soon as those words left my mouth, it was as if the Lord Himself spoke to me with the words from the scripture, "The joy of the Lord is your STRENGTH" (Nehemiah 8:10) So, I changed my prayer and prayed, "Lord, give me your joy!" As soon as those words left my mouth, it was as if the Lord Himself spoke to me again with the words from the scripture, "In His presence is fulness of JOY." (Psalm 16:11) So, one last time, I changed my prayer and prayed, "Lord, help me to get into Your Presence."

Just think, there is no more meaningful prayer that we can pray in our lives than a simple prayer of seeking God's presence. Every need is met in His presence! Where is the one place where God's presence is fully manifested? Isn't it Heaven? Are there any needs in Heaven? Are there any who are weak or sickly? Sad or depressed? Overtaken by struggles? NO! And, this is why Jesus told us to pray, "Your will be done on Earth as it is in HEAVEN [the place of God's Presence]." So, when we pray those words we are actually praying, "Lord, may your presence come invade our lives." His Earthly presence in our lives conquers every need we have, even as His Heavenly Presence will not permit or allow neediness or weakness.

Got a need in your life today? Seek God's presence… every need is met there!

My Prayer for Today:
"Lord, I need strength! But not just any strength… I need YOUR strength! I know that it can only be found in YOUR presence, so I will spend time today seeking Your presence, because in Your presence is fulness of Joy… and Your joy gives me the strength I need!"

Psalm 140:13
Surely the righteous shall give thanks unto thy name: the upright shall dwell in thy presence.

TODAY'S FOOD FOR THOUGHT
Exodus 14:14 tells us
"The LORD will fight for you WHILE YOU KEEP SILENT."
I wonder if He fights for us while we're verbally defending ourselves?

FOR THOSE WHO LOVE GOD
February 11 | August 11

I don't know why it's taken me so long to see this, but I've recently come to realize that there are two sets of promises found in the Scriptures. There are promises that are ours simply because *God Loves Us*, but there is also a set of promises that belong to *Those Who Love God*.

For instance, everyone knows John 3:16 "For God so loved... that He gave His only son... that we might have eternal life." The gift of eternal life is AVAILABLE to us because of "God's Love for Us."

There are other scriptures, however, that offer God's promises with the prerequisite that "We Love Him." I've quoted the promise of Romans 8:28 much of my life without fully appreciating or comprehending what it says. It tells us that "All things work together for good.... TO THOSE WHO LOVE GOD". Not to those "whom God loves" (that would be everybody). What a blessing to know that nothing can come my way except for that which is completely FOR MY GOOD! But, the condition of that promise must be met first... I must LOVE GOD.

I'm thankful that He loves me! But, to gain the full benefit of being in relationship with God, the love needs to be reciprocated. Here are a few other promises that remind us that there are special promises for those "WHO LOVE GOD."

1.) James 1:12 (NIV) "Blessed is the one who perseveres under trial because, having stood the test, that person will receive the crown of life that the Lord has promised TO THOSE WHO LOVE HIM.

2.) 1 Corinthians 2:9 (KJV) "Eye hath not seen, nor ear heard, neither have entered into the heart of man, the things which God hath prepared FOR THEM THAT LOVE HIM."

3.) Psalm 145:20 (NLT) "The LORD protects all those WHO LOVE HIM, but he destroys the wicked.

4.) Daniel 9:4 (NIV) "I prayed to the LORD my God and confessed: "Lord, the great and awesome God, who keeps his covenant of love with THOSE WHO LOVE HIM and keep his commandments."

TODAY'S WISDOM NUGGET
NO GOD INPUT = NO GOOD OUTPUT.

WALK... BY FAITH
February 12 | August 12

2 Corinthians 5:7 says, "For we WALK by faith, not by sight." One day, out of curiosity, I looked up the definition of the word WALK.

WALK: move at a regular and fairly slow pace by lifting and setting down each foot in turn, never having both feet off the ground at once.

That last phrase captured my attention: "Never having both feet off the ground at once." I guess I never thought about it in that way before, but when you walk there's always one foot on the ground. Unlike running or jumping where both feet leave the ground for a moment of time... and unlike standing still, where both feet never leave the ground.

So the scripture says *walk by faith*. It doesn't say *run by faith*... not *jump by faith*... not *stand by faith*. (Although we do stand "IN" faith). What's my point? Walking is MOVEMENT IN A DIRECTION, AT A SLOW PACE... AND ONE FOOT IS ALWAYS ON THE GROUND. We are moving in a direction, towards God's kingdom, BY FAITH. It is a slow, gradual pace. We are never fully committed to Earth, because one foot is always off the ground (in the invisible realm). We realize that we are "on Earth" but we don't place all of our hope and trust in it. That's why we never commit to putting both feet on the ground at the same time. That would make Earth our foundation. Earth is not our foundation... God is!

Neither do we ever take both feet off the ground in our movement towards God's heavenly kingdom. We are connected to Earth when we walk. We always have one foot on the ground. As Faith People we impact this earth by staying connected to it, by praying for its people, and by being "salt and light" in a "bland and dark" world.

So, today, remember that our WALK of faith has us moving. We're moving in God's direction... one foot connected to Earth... one foot committed to the air, connected to the invisible realm where God is at work, and where miracles happen!

1 John 5:4 - This is the victory that overcometh the world, even our faith.

TODAY'S FOOD FOR THOUGHT
Though I'm AMAZED by the fast-growth of the weed, I'm FED by the slow-growth of the vegetable vine.

YOU ARE NOT YOUR OWN
February 13 | August 13

One night, my friend Mario and I got into a discussion about tattoos. He showed me a half-finished tattoo that he had on his arm. When I asked why it didn't get completed he told me this interesting story....

Many years ago, in his B.C. (Before Christ) years, Mario was serving time in prison. One of his fellow inmates was a tattoo artist. He started on Mario's tattoo and got called away in the middle of working on it. He promised to come back and finish it later. But, while he was away, someone snitched on his "illegal" operation. He was put in solitary confinement for 30 days, and his tattoo paraphernalia was confiscated. When I asked why he was sent to solitary confinement Mario replied, "When you're a prisoner you are property of the state, so putting a tattoo on a prisoner is considered to be defacing state property." Talk about a moment of "revelation" for me! When he said those words I immediately thought of the verse in Corinthians that says, "Do you not know that you are the temple of the Holy Spirit, who is in you, whom you have received from God? You are not your own; You were bought with a price." (1 Corinthians 6:19-20)

Friend, if you are a Christian your body is not your own... you have been bought with a price. This is not about tattoos, necessarily, but it is about the way we live our lives and the things we do to our bodies, thinking that our bodies belong to us. Just three chapters before 1 Corinthians 6, mentioned above, it says, "If any man defile the temple of God [our body], him shall God destroy; for the temple of God is holy, which temple ye are." (1 Corinthians 3:17) We talk about our bodies like they are ours and that's just not true... they belong to God... He purchased us.

Of course all of what I just said only applies to a person who is a Christian... someone who claims that they BELONG to Christ. God has the final say about what I do "to" and "with" my body. It's not my decision anymore. So many of our life's problems could be remedied by just reminding ourselves of this truth. I am not my own, I have been bought with a price; therefore I must glorify God in my body and in my spirit, which belongs to God. (1 Corinthians 6:20)

TODAY'S FOOD FOR THOUGHT
I'd rather be humbled on this side of eternity than the other.
Humble yourselves before the Lord, and he will lift you up. James 4:10

STANDING IN THE GAP
February 14 | August 14

I was sitting in my living room one afternoon when I saw a FedEx truck pull up in front of my house. When the driver got out and opened the back door to his truck a strange thought popped into my head. I thought within myself, "I wonder if this guy has anyone in his life that is praying for him?" As I had that thought a scripture verse came up inside me: "I looked for a man to stand in the gap...." (Ezekiel 22:30). I determined at that moment to quietly pray for that young man, that God would bless him and his family, that he would be safe and protected, and that he would find success in his life.

There may be people you meet today who don't have a single soul praying for them. No one is standing in the gap between Heaven and hell, between life and death, between success and failure, lifting them before the Father in Heaven, seeking His blessing for them. I know the reason I'm blessed, healthy and experiencing abundance is because someone "stood in the gap" for me when I didn't have even the smallest spiritual inclination inside me. Someone else's prayers upheld me.

It's an awesome thing that a devoted Christian can do for his or her world. To see a random stranger on the street and say a prayer for them. To reach Heaven in their behalf. To stand in the gap, even though that person has no idea of the intercession going on for them. I don't mind telling you, there was a certain sense of satisfaction I experienced as I reflected on the thought that my prayer for this young man might be the very thing that keeps him safe during the next season of his life. He might have been in a downward spiral that morning when he woke up, but that afternoon prayer was lifted to Heaven for him... prayer that can bring change to his life.

What a blessing to be one of God's "secret agents." What a blessing to know that I can make a difference in my world by quietly praying for those around me... for people who aren't even aware that I exist... much less that I am standing in the gap for them.

Isaiah 59:16
And he saw that there was no man, and wondered that there was no intercessor.

TODAY'S WISDOM NUGGET
If you have energy and strength enough to complain, you're wasting it.

WORDS CAN BE POWERFUL!
February 15 | August 15

One winter morning I injured my toe while playing racquetball with some friends. Although I was in quite a bit of pain, I continued to play through to the end of our match. When I got home I went back to my office and started back with my work and regular activities. I guess it was around 6 o'clock that evening that I decided to inspect my toe a little more closely. It had swollen up, the skin was tight and it had turned black and blue on the bottom. I thought to myself, "I think I've broken my toe!" I showed it to my wife and she said, "It looks broken to me." When she said those words I instantly felt faint. When I regained my composure I began to laugh. My wife said, "What are you laughing about?" I said, "Because I just started feeling faint when you said 'It looks broken to me.'" I was amazed at how my physical body reacted when I heard those words! I hadn't felt faint the whole time I was enduring the pain in my toe while I played racquetball or while I was working at my desk for several hours, but then just 5 words were spoken and I almost passed out! Don't tell me that words aren't powerful!

I've heard words before that have empowered me, and encouraged me to press on during a difficult endeavor. I have also heard words that have drained me of my strength and my "will to go on." Words can be powerful!

I've heard words that have made me joyful and glad to be alive. I have also heard words that made me sad and depressed. Words can be powerful!

I've heard words that made me want to fight a good fight against my enemy, the devil. I've also heard words that caused me to fear and want to raise the white flag of surrender during the battles of life. Words can be powerful!

God created the world by using words. We create our world by using words. Words can be powerful!

Proverbs 18:21
Death and Life are in the POWER of the tongue.

TODAY'S FOOD FOR THOUGHT
If you can't control yourself somebody else will.
"A person without self-control is like a city with broken-down walls"
Proverbs 25:28

IT'S ALL ABOUT BREATH
February 16 | August 16

In the beginning God created man out of a handful of dirt. But the man was not alive until God INSPIRED (meaning, breathed into) him. So God INSPIRED man, and man became a living being, and lived in a garden called Eden with his wife. (Genesis 2:7)

There was a serpent who also lived in the garden of Eden. Along came Satan and he CONSPIRED (meaning, breathed together) with the serpent to deceive the newly formed man and his wife. (Genesis 3:1)

Because man disobeyed God's command to not partake of the forbidden fruit, God put a curse on the work of man's hands and said that he would PERSPIRE (meaning, breathe out through the skin) from his hard labor on the Earth all the days of his life. (Genesis 3:19)

Man was no longer INSPIRED (meaning, breathed into)! But, God had a plan to restore man back to good relationship. He sent His son to Earth to die for man's transgression.

After Jesus had died on the cross and rose from the dead He met with his disciples in a house and RESPIRED (meaning, to breathe again) upon them and said "Receive ye the Holy Ghost." When Jesus did this man was once again INSPIRED. (John 20:22)

So, in a nutshell, this is how everything TRANSPIRED.......

- God INSPIRED us
- Satan CONSPIRED against us
- As a result man PERSPIRED
- Jesus RESPIRED upon us
- We receive the Holy Spirit so we can once again be INSPIRED.

I'm INSPIRED...how about you?

TODAY'S FOOD FOR THOUGHT

Ever heard the phrase "Let him speak now or forever HOLD HIS PEACE"? Did you know you have a peace that you carry with you? And, when you refrain from speaking you are "holding your peace." Sometimes, peace can be found simply by keeping your mouth shut.

WHAT CHANGED?
February 17 | August 17

I was teaching at the Men's Home Bible Study from John 9, where Jesus healed the blind beggar. God dropped it into my heart to ask one simple question… "What changed for the man when Jesus healed him of his blindness?" I wasn't even sure myself of all the ways the question could be answered. The guys began to answer that question with their own thoughts and opinions. They had some great insights. There was the obvious answer, "He could see things that he had never seen before," but then came other answers like, "He no longer needed other people to guide him," and, "He became a testimony of Jesus' healing power."

Then the answer God wanted me to see when He prompted me to ask the question finally came to me. I asked the guys, "What was the blind man doing when Jesus first met him?" They replied, "He was begging." So, I asked, "Was there a need for the man to beg any longer after Jesus healed him of his blindness?" They replied, "No!"

You see, Jesus didn't just HEAL the man of his blindness… HE HEALED HIS LIFE! The only way this man could survive as a blind man was by begging. But, when he received sight he was then able to be a contributing member of society… to work a job… to take care of his own personal needs and welfare. Blindness had robbed him of these dignities.

Jesus doesn't heal a man's life so he can just go back and be the beggar he was. He brings a life change that becomes evident to all who have seen and known that man. This is the good news of the gospel. Jesus heals us and gives us back our ability to be "givers" instead of "takers." He restores our dignity so that we're no longer beggars, barely getting by and depending on others to meet our needs. Had there been a "rest of the story" about this blind beggar whom Jesus healed, we know one thing for sure: He would have no longer been called BLIND… or BEGGAR!

Psalm 37:25
I have been young, and now am old; yet have I not seen the righteous forsaken, nor his seed begging bread.

TODAY'S WISDOM NUGGET
Sometimes the truth can make you feel bad, and a lie can make you feel good. But only the truth can set you free. Forget about feelings!

WAIT
February 18 | August 18

Isaiah 40:31
They that WAIT upon the Lord shall renew their strength

For the longest time I misunderstood the meaning of WAIT as it appears in the verse above. I thought it meant to "sit patiently and do nothing in anticipation of something that is about to happen." But, a deeper meaning to the word WAIT came to me as I was sitting in a restaurant one day and my glass of tea was almost empty. I was just about to look for the server to request a refill of my glass of tea when, from out of nowhere, the server appeared with a pitcher of tea, picked my glass up off the table and refilled it to the brim. The words "I need more tea" never had to cross my lips because someone was WAITING on me. That's why they're called WAITERS and WAITRESSES. They anticipate the needs of the people they are attending and serve them when the smallest need arises. Suddenly, the words "WAIT upon the Lord" gained a fresh new meaning for me.

Now I understand that the word WAIT is not passive... it is active. I am one who WAITS UPON THE LORD. I am the Lord's "server" (servant). I am to be attentive to the needs of His kingdom, and to anticipate what my next actions should be to be pleasing to the One I am serving. And, just like a person who has been served with excellence by a proficient WAITER will reward that WAITER with a healthy tip, even so, the Lord rewards those who WAIT UPON HIM with a much needed benefit... RENEWED STRENGTH.

My Confession for Today:
I'm WAITING on the Lord. I'm attentive to the needs of His kingdom and His people. When I see a need I respond quickly because I'm paying attention... just like a good WAITER!

Psalm 27:14 (NAS)
Wait for the LORD; Be strong and let your heart take courage; Yes, wait for the LORD.

TODAY'S WORD OF EXHORTATION
There are two kinds of people in this life: Those who remind us of life's realities and those who remind us of life's possibilities. Be a "possibilites" person!

SELAH!
February 19 | August 19

One autumn morning when I woke up, the first thing I did was peek through the blinds to see what the morning looked like. I was stunned by the colors of one of the most beautiful sunrises I had ever seen. I looked at the clock. It was 6:36am. Hurriedly, I got my clothes on, grabbed my camera and ran to the end of my street to an open field where I could take photos of the beautiful sunrise. By the time I had gotten to the open field the fiery red and orange had already begun to fade to a pale orange and yellow. I took a few photos... I looked at my watch... it was 6:41.

Five Minutes! That's all it took for the beauty of that moment to fade away. I had moved as quickly as possible, and nearly missed it completely. A beautiful moment had come and gone in just FIVE MINUTES and I took it in as best I could.

Life is full of "beautiful moments." But, our lives move at such a rapid pace that we oftentimes miss out on these beautiful moments. Sometimes we sleep through them. Sometimes we see them and aren't aware of how beautiful they are. Sometimes we pass right by them, but are distracted by other less important things, or even worse, we get distracted by things that are downright ugly (like the evening news, for instance).

There is a word used in the book of Psalms "SELAH" that theologians believe means "Pause and reflect for a moment." So few of us know how to "pause and reflect" any more. We go from one thing to the next, seamlessly... not taking in the full beauty of the moment that just passed us by. I'm as guilty as the next guy.

"Lord, help us today to pause and reflect... to have a SELAH moment where we admire the beauty around us... where we don't entertain the negative and the ugly... where we give our complete attention to the beauty around us."

Psalm 32:7
You are my hiding place; you will protect me from trouble and surround me with songs of deliverance. "Selah"

TODAY'S WORD OF EXHORTATION
Forgive like your own forgiveness depended on it... because it does.
"Forgive, and you will be forgiven." Luke 6:37

TASTING DEATH
February 20 | August 20

In Hebrews 2:9 it says that Jesus "tasted death for every man." What do you suppose death tastes like? Guess what... You'll never have to find out because Jesus tasted death for you! He TASTED DEATH FOR EVERY MAN!

In Bible times, a king would have a servant called a "cup-bearer" and this person would taste the king's wine and other drinks before it ever came to the king's lips. If the drink had been poisoned by an enemy or someone who wanted to overthrow the king the cup-bearer would be the one to die from the poison... not the king. The cup-bearer, in essence, was TASTING DEATH for the king, so the king's life could be preserved and protected.

As Jesus prayed in the Garden of Gethsemane he prayed a prayer that most of us are familiar with: "O my Father, if it be possible, let this cup pass from me: nevertheless not as I will, but as thou wilt." (Matthew 26:39) What was the "cup" Jesus spoke of? It was the cup He was about to drink from for all of mankind... THE CUP OF SUFFERING AND DEATH. Jesus became our Cup-Bearer!

Today, those who are children of God should not fear death, for we shall not taste of its horror... Jesus tasted it for us! Let's give thanks today for this fact... that Jesus considered us to be KINGS in the sight of God, and that He took on the form of a lowly servant, THE CUP-BEARER, to preserve our lives.

Hebrews 2:9
But we see Jesus, who was made a little lower than the angels for the suffering of death, crowned with glory and honour; that he by the grace of God should taste death for every man.

I Corinthians 15:54-55
So when this corruptible shall have put on incorruption, and this mortal shall have put on immortality, then shall be brought to pass the saying that is written, Death is swallowed up in victory. O death, where is thy sting? O grave, where is thy victory?

TODAY'S WISDOM NUGGET
Life lesson learned from an old tree:
"You never realize how many dead branches you have on you
until a storm blows through."

ENCOURAGE YOURSELF
February 21 | August 21

Years ago I used to be a critic of "faith" people, and people who spouted off "positive confessions" all the time. To be sure there has been some abuse and misuse in this area, but in more recent years I have repented of my criticisms... out of necessity more than anything else. You see, there are some mornings I wake up (just like today) and I feel absolutely terrible. Depression is standing at my front door, knocking repeatedly, wanting to make itself "at home" in me. I don't have a medication that I can take to defeat it... I don't have a "life coach" that I can turn to for encouragement... if I read the morning news for some comfort all I find is bad news. I have a choice to make in these situations: I can succumb to the depression that hovers over me, or I can battle against it by speaking words of encouragement to myself. I choose the latter!

I refuse to let depression and hopelessness rule over me, so I encourage myself with uplifting scriptures like "I can do all things through Christ who gives me strength" and "Greater is He that is in me than he that is in the world." Today, one particular scripture that came to mind was "God is our refuge and strength, a very present help in trouble." (Psalm 46:1) After speaking this verse over my life a few times this morning, I felt encouraged and ready to take on the day. Positive words in my mouth became my "medication" to defeat depression... God's Spirit became my "life coach"... and God's Word became the "good news" that I needed to get me pepped up for a new day.

Some may criticize me for being a positive thinker and a "faith" person. They might think that I'm "in denial" or "not facing reality," but if they could see the person I would be without these positive scriptural affirmations in my life I think they'd agree that I'm a better, happier person because of it.

1 Samuel 30:6
And David was greatly distressed; for the people spake of stoning him, because the soul of all the people was grieved... but David ENCOURAGED HIMSELF in the Lord his God.

TODAY'S FOOD FOR THOUGHT
The Lord is good and His mercy endures forever.
How long does yours last?

58

THE FIRST TIME
February 22 | August 22

I asked a young boy in my elementary class at church to ask the blessing over our supper. He said he didn't want to do it. When I asked why he didn't want to say the prayer he said, "Because, I've never prayed in front of people before." When he said that I was taken back to the first time I ever prayed "out loud" in front of a group of people.

I was 14 years old, in a Sunday School class with a bunch of people I didn't know, in a church that I was visiting with a friend. The Sunday School teacher asked that everybody in the classroom say a word of prayer as we went around the room. I was scared to death! When it was my turn to pray all I could say was, "Lord, bless everyone in this room here, today, Amen." Short, sweet, and nervously spoken… my very first prayer ever spoken out loud where others could hear.

I told my story to the boy and the rest of my class. I told the little boy, "There's a first time for everything you do in life. Tonight can be your first time to pray in front of a group of people just like I did it all those years ago. Once you've gotten your first time out of the way, you'll finally be free from the fear of doing it for the first time." After my short word of encouragement, the little boy agreed to pray for the meal. He did an excellent job of formulating his words and saying what was on his heart. His first time to pray out loud in front of people was over… a fear had been overcome! He was now free to pray out loud in front of other people.

Life is full of first time experiences. For some reason we seem to think that they only happen when we're young, but that's just not true. There are first time experiences awaiting us every day of our lives if we will open ourselves up to them. The only thing that separates us from those experiences is fear. Life gets old and stale when we stay in our comfort zones and fail to embrace the new FIRST TIME experiences that are all around us.

Challenge for Today: Try something new, for the first time… even if it means ordering something new off the restaurant menu. Refuse to be held by the thought that there are no more new experiences to discover. Overcome the fear of "THE FIRST TIME."

TODAY'S WISDOM NUGGET
When your patience is being tested, remember this:
You're worth your WAIT in gold!

GOD IS NOT...

February 23 | August 23

FICKLE: He doesn't love you today and then have nothing to do with you tomorrow... His love is constant and enduring. (Jeremiah 31:3 "I have loved you with an EVERLASTING LOVE.)

PARTIAL: He doesn't show favoritism to one person and overlook you because you don't "measure up." We all have the same potential and possibilities for success given to us by the same Father... differences are only manifested by our own ability to grasp and receive all that He has for us. (Psalm 99:4 "Mighty King, lover of justice, you have established fairness.")

LIMITED: God doesn't have a limited supply of power or love that he divides out among those who call upon His Name. In the Bible, His supply is described with words such as abundant, overflowing, abounding and generous. (Jeremiah 32:17 "Ah Lord GOD! Behold, You have made the heavens and the earth by Your great power and by Your outstretched arm! Nothing is too difficult for You.")

EXPIRING: There is not an expiration date on any of God's promises. Promises that were made 2,000 years ago are still accessible to those who will receive them by faith. The passing of time has no impact on God or His Promises. (Psalm 105:8 "He hath remembered his covenant for ever, the word which he commanded to a thousand generations.")

ANTIQUATED: Sure, He's been around for thousands and thousands of years (an eternity, to be exact) but He is NOT OLD. Yes, humans grow OLD through the passing of time, but that is not the case with God. He is not "Stuck in the Past" trying to relive His glory days. He is always doing something NEW and FRESH. Jeremiah says that His mercies are "NEW every morning" (Lamentations 3:23). Revelation 21:1 reports that in the future He will make a NEW HEAVEN and a NEW EARTH. Then, just a couple of verses later, God says "Behold, I am making ALL THINGS NEW." (Revelation 21:5) No, God is not out-dated, or old-fashioned... He's always on the cutting edge of what is NEW.

TODAY'S FOOD FOR THOUGHT

If you're ever asked the question "If God is Love, why does He let innocent people die?" ask this question in reply "If God IS NOT Love, why did He let innocent Jesus die?" John 3:16

SAY WHAT JESUS SAID
February 24 | August 24

I was talking to a lady one Saturday afternoon who had visited the Holy Land. Now, that's something that I think would be really inspiring… to actually WALK WHERE JESUS WALKED. Just imagining that the very place I was standing might have been the very place that Jesus stood and preached, taught or healed someone… what an incredibly, inspiring thought.

When the lady told me of the souvenirs she had purchased on her trip to the Holy Land I remembered the time I purchased a true Bible artifact at a traveling Bible exhibit. It was a "mite" from Jesus' day that had been excavated in the Holy Land (like the Widow's Mite from the Gospel Story). The reason I bought it? It was just the thought of being able to HOLD SOMETHING THAT JESUS MIGHT HAVE HELD in His hand.

Yes, to WALK WHERE JESUS WALKED and to HOLD WHAT JESUS HELD… what an awesome thought!!

As I was thinking along these lines, this thought came to me: You may not be able to WALK WHERE JESUS WALKED, or HOLD WHAT JESUS HELD, but you can always SAY WHAT JESUS SAID (because we have His words written in the Bible) and that should affect us and inspire us more than anything else! Just think, when you say the Lord's Prayer "Our Father which art in Heaven, hallowed be thy name…" you are saying the very same words that came from Jesus' lips! What an incredible thought! None of His words were impotent or random… they were powerful and full of meaning. When I speak His words I'm not just rehearsing a part of history, I'm also impacting my current situations with His life-transforming words... and that's the most awe-inspiring thought of all!

Luke 4:22 (NIV)
All spoke well of him and were amazed at the gracious words that came from his lips.

TODAY'S FOOD FOR THOUGHT
Check out this King James Bible word: LOVINGKINDNESS. It's not used in a lot of modern translations. That's regrettable! Instead, it is replaced with the word "love." Unfortunately, these days you can say that you LOVE without being KIND. We all need a little more lovingKINDNESS. *"Thy lovingkindness is better than life."* Psalm 63:3

WHAT DOES THE WORD "DIE" MEAN?

February 25 | August 25

God has a different definition for the word "DIE" than we do. He told Adam and Eve that if they ate of the Tree of Knowledge of Good and Evil that they would "surely DIE." We think DIE means when the heart stops beating, the brain stops sending and receiving nerve impulses, and the lungs stop breathing. When Adam and Eve ate the forbidden fruit, none of that happened, but they did DIE, because God said they would. If anyone knows what the word DIE means it has to be God! So, Adam and Eve DIED but they were still walking around, lungs breathing, heart beating, brain thinking and seemingly alive... yet they were DEAD.

Thousands of years went by and Jesus appeared on the scene. He made an incredible statement right before He raised His friend Lazarus from the dead. He said, "Whoever lives and believes in me shall NEVER DIE." He said those words to Martha. She believed in Him, yet several years later her body was buried in a grave. In our eyes she DIED. But Jesus said that she would NEVER DIE if she believed in Him. So, you have to ask yourself this question, "Did Jesus tell a lie... or do we just not understand what the word DIE means?" I think we can all agree that Jesus didn't lie, so our definition of the word DIE needs to change.

I believe in Jesus, therefore, I will NEVER DIE. One day they will bury my body in a grave, but I will NEVER DIE because Jesus said I wouldn't. So, I've come to this conclusion: It is not in our bodies where we experience the meaning of the word DIE... it is in our soul and spirit. This body will one day cease activity on earth... people may weep and mourn at my grave... but I won't be DEAD because I believe in Jesus, and He said I would never DIE.

James 2:26 (NIV)
As the body without the spirit is dead, so faith without deeds is dead.

TODAY'S WORD OF ENCOURAGEMENT
I'm not a "Has Been"
'Cause God is the "I Am,"
And if the "I Am" is in me
That means I'm a "Will Be."
Beloved, now we are children of God, and it has not appeared as yet what we WILL BE. - 1 John 3:2

BEING LOVED VS. BEING PLEASING
February 26 | August 26

Matthew 3:17 (NIV)
(God speaking of Jesus at His Baptism)
And a voice from heaven said, "This is my Son, whom I LOVE; with him I am well PLEASED."

Matthew 17:5 (NIV)
(God speaking of Jesus on the Mount of Transfiguration)
"This is my Son, whom I LOVE; with him I am well PLEASED."

There are only 3 recorded instances of the voice of God being heard during Jesus' ministry. The 2 scriptures above are 2 of the instances. In both instances, God repeats the same phrase "This is my Son, whom I LOVE; with him I am well PLEASED." You can quickly read over those words and not see that there is a distinction between being LOVED by God and being PLEASING to Him. JESUS DID BOTH! The question I ask is: "Do WE want to do both?"

Everyone likes the idea that God LOVES them unconditionally no matter what their lifestyle, sin, upbringing, imperfections, etc., etc. But, there are two questions we must ask ourselves: "Is God PLEASED with me" and "Do I want to be PLEASING to Him?"

God's LOVE for us is entirely dependent upon His own ability to love even the most unloveable. Our works, our faith, and even our reciprocation of His love are not a part of the equation. His LOVE is unconditional! But us being PLEASING to Him is dependent upon our personal desire to obey Him and His Word. Everyone is LOVED by God... but not everyone is PLEASING. I find this idea very challenging! I'm thankful He LOVES me... now I want to PLEASE HIM.

2 Corinthians 5:9 (NIV)
So we make it our goal to please him.

Hebrews 11:6 (NIV)
And without faith it is impossible to please God.

TODAY'S FOOD FOR THOUGHT
I've met two kinds of sad people: 1.) People who are cursed... and they realize it. 2.) People who are blessed... and they don't realize it.

EVERYTHING THE LIGHT TOUCHES
February 27 | August 27

One warm summer morning while I was on my morning walk, I took a moment to watch rays of sunlight illuminate patches of ground around me as beams of light made their way through openings in the trees. As I was standing there appreciating the warmth and color that the light was bringing, in my head and heart I heard a phrase from the movie *The Lion King* that somehow stayed with me. In the movie, as the morning sun was rising, Mufasa was showing little Simba the Lion's territory. Mufasa said, "Everything that the light touches is our kingdom." That's the phrase I heard in my heart and head, just as if God Himself was speaking it to me.

"EVERYTHING THE LIGHT TOUCHES IS OUR KINGDOM!" That's what God says to His children (His princes and princesses). 1 John says that "if we walk in the LIGHT as He is in the light then we have fellowship with one another, and the blood of Jesus cleanses us from all our sin." We are guaranteed success in this life as we walk in the light because EVERYTHING THE LIGHT TOUCHES IS OUR KINGDOM. But when we venture into the darkness, into the realm and territory of our enemy (the devil), there are no guarantees for our success or blessing.

Sometimes people wonder why they are experiencing misfortune and failure on every turn and don't realize it is because they have ventured away from "The Light" and are walking in darkness. 1 John 1:6 tells us that "if we say we have fellowship with Him and yet walk in darkness, we lie and do not practice the truth." It's impossible to walk in the Light and in Darkness at the same time. For the child of God, success comes from walking in the Light... because EVERYTHING THE LIGHT TOUCHES IS OUR KINGDOM.

My Prayer for Today:
"Lord, teach me to walk in the LIGHT where my success is guaranteed."

Psalm 119:105 (NIV)
Your word is a lamp for my feet, a light on my path.

TODAY'S WISDOM NUGGET
I'd rather be blessed than rich, and here's why:
blessings can make you rich, but riches can't make you blessed.
"It is the blessing of the LORD that makes rich..." Proverbs 10:22 NAS

BE SALT AND LIGHT
February 28 | August 28

I was having lunch with a friend at a local restaurant. As is usually the case when the two of us get together, before we knew it our conversation had turned to the Bible and the good things of God. We had a good time discussing Bible truths and gleaning from each other's studies and revelations.

When we left the restaurant and were heading to our cars in the parking lot a lady exited the restaurant not far behind us and called out to us. She said, "Excuse me... I'm sorry for eavesdropping but I was sitting in the booth next to you and I couldn't help but overhear your conversation. That really blessed me a lot!" She went on to say, "I was especially interested in what you were saying about Heaven. My mother died one year ago today and when I heard you talking about Heaven I couldn't help but think about her, because I know that's where she is right now." Her eyes began to tear up… mine did too. She thanked us for helping make the anniversary of her mother's death just a little less sad, and then said, "I better go back into the restaurant before they think I've left without paying!"

Now, to be honest, our reference to Heaven in our conversation was for just a brief 30 second period. It wasn't our main topic of discussion. But, it was just enough to minister to the heart of a grieving daughter on that day. God knows just how to use our words and actions, even in the smallest of ways, to minister to hurting and broken people. You never know when something as simple as a dinner conversation can be a blessing to someone else. Keep being "salt" and "light" wherever you go… you may be ministering to someone without even knowing it.

Romans 1:16 (NIV)
For I am not ashamed of the gospel, because it is the power of God that brings salvation to everyone who believes.

TODAY'S WISDOM NUGGET
A tight grip can save your life... or kill you. Holding on tight to a
rope dangling from a cliff makes that rope a lifeline. But, holding on
tight to an anchor rope can plunge you to a watery grave.
Holding on tight to anger, fear, unforgiveness and hurt will only drag
you down. Hold on tight to Jesus... your lifeline.

STAY!
March 1 | August 29

On one of my morning walks I was trying to teach my dog, Archie, to SIT and STAY before crossing the street as an oncoming car approached. He was sitting as he had been commanded, but as soon as the approaching car got right beside us, Archie jetted out into the street. If not for my tight grip on his leash he would have been run over! Later, on our return back to the house, we had another opportunity to practice SIT and STAY as a large truck was making its way toward us. I told Archie, "Sit" and then I said, "Stay, Stay, Stay"… repeating the command over and over again. He did much better this next time and didn't move until I said, "Okay".

To be honest, even though he did better, I didn't consider it a success. The reason? Because I had to repeat the command STAY so many times. Do you know what the command STAY means? It means, "Remain where you are until you receive your next command." Eventually, Archie will have to learn that the command STAY need only be spoken once.

Archie doesn't have a full grasp of the word STAY yet. I'm not so sure I do either. My Master has given me the command to STAY in Him and in His Word, and to ABIDE under the shadow of His wings. Sometimes I get anxious and am waiting for the next command from the Lord when the last one He gave was STAY. There is holding power in that command. STAYING somewhere is difficult when you see others moving here and there, doing as they please, and making decisions, sometimes without even seeking God's direction. But, honestly, the best place you can be in life is the place He told you to STAY. So, here I am today, in the place He told me to STAY… under the shadow of His wings.

Psalm 91:1
He that dwelleth [stays] in the secret place of the Most High shall ABIDE under the shadow of the Almighty.

YOUR SMILE FOR TODAY

A number 2 pencil makes a bold, dark mark during its lifetime, but it's not too proud to admit it can make a mistake, so it carries a pink eraser with it everywhere it goes. A ball-point pen, on the other hand, seems to be way too sure of itself and it's abilities. When it does make a mistake the correction can be very ugly. BE A NUMBER 2 PENCIL!

WAS THAT GOD'S PURPOSE FOR MY LIFE?
March 2 | August 30

One summer morning during my morning prayer walk I prayed, "Lord, make every moment of this day count in my life. May I be connected to Your purpose and plan for my life throughout this day." Less than 5 minutes later I was met by a lost German Shepherd dog. The next several hours of my day were devoted to trying to find the dog's owners. As I sat in the back of my truck while my son drove me and the lost dog around nearby neighborhoods, I thought to myself, "So, is this the answer to the prayer I prayed? Am I connecting to God's purpose and plan for me?"

None of MY work got accomplished. MY schedule was shot. I was completely out of MY routine. I knocked on doors, talked to total strangers, and even went to the police department, just so I could help a lost dog find his home. A man from the animal shelter finally came by at 4:00pm to take the dog, and assured me that he would either find the dog's owner or find him a good home, since he was such a beautiful dog. When he left I realized that I had just spent my entire day centered around a lost dog.

The next morning, as I reflected on the prayer I prayed the previous day about being connected to God's purpose for my life, I asked the Lord, "Was that really your purpose for my life, yesterday?" Here's what I heard spoken to my heart:

> "You cared about something that wasn't your own... that's part of God's purpose for your life. You showed compassion on one who couldn't return the favor... that's part of God's purpose for your life. You tried to help the homeless find a home... that's part of God's purpose for your life. You took care of "the lost"... that's part of God's purpose for your life.

Yes, I know, it was "just a dog." But God was teaching me that the art of compassion connects us to His heart and purpose. Any time our heart is moved with compassion to help another individual (even a lost dog) we are experiencing part of God's plan for our lives... we are connecting with His heart, and our heart expands in the process.

Matthew 25:35 - "I was a stranger, and ye took me in"

TODAY'S WISDOM NUGGET
If you love beauty be prepared to fight ugly.

THE VOICE OF OUR ENEMY
March 3 | August 31

In the late summer of 2015, I found a baby dove during my morning prayer walk and decided to take him home and care for him. Raising an orphaned baby dove in a house with 2 bird-eating cats was an interesting challenge. The baby dove was sitting in a basket next to my computer while I was working one morning. One of our cats was in the house eating breakfast and let out a loud "Meow." Immediately, the little bird's head popped up from the basket as if to say, "What was that!" I looked at the baby bird and said, "That's the voice of your enemy!" It lowered its head back down and eventually drifted back off to sleep. That little bird had no idea the amount of danger I had kept it from, and most likely didn't connect the "voice" that he heard as being any kind of threat to him.

Just like that baby bird, we have no idea the amount of danger that God has kept us from as He has sheltered us from our hungry enemy. The Bible says that our enemy, the devil, goes around like a ROARING LION [making his voice known], seeking whom he may devour (1 Peter 5:8). Satan would like nothing better than to turn us into "lunch meat," but if we are wise to the VOICE OF OUR ENEMY we can overcome him as we stay sheltered under the Shadow of the Almighty.

But, the question is: "Do we recognize the voice of our enemy?" When we hear him say, "Go ahead and do what God told you not to do," and we follow his voice (just like Adam and Eve did) destruction is imminent. When we hear that voice whisper in our ear, "God can't help you through this" or "This is a hopeless situation" do we understand that is our enemy trying to steal our faith in our Loving, Powerful Father? It is a voice that should be rebuked and quieted… not allowed to continue to speak… it should be resisted at all cost! It is the VOICE OF OUR ENEMY!

John 10:10 (NAS)
The thief comes only to steal and kill and destroy; I came that they may have life, and have it abundantly.

TODAY'S WORD OF ENCOURAGEMENT
Hello Child of God! Has anyone called you "Majestic" lately?
"As for the saints who are in the earth, They are the MAJESTIC ones in whom is all my delight." Psalm 16:3 NAS

YOU'RE JUST GONNA HAVE TO FORGET ABOUT THAT
March 4 | September 1

My dog, Archie, and I were returning home from our walk one morning and, as usual, Archie was pulling on his leash trying to get out ahead of me. Suddenly, without any warning, he took a detour from the pathway as if being pulled by an unseen force. Actually, it really was an unseen force… he had caught the scent of something in the air and was running in all directions trying to find the source. He was pulling on the leash, yanking me in one direction and then another. I let him have about 30 seconds to investigate but then I said to him, "You're just gonna have to forget about that" as I jerked him back onto the path and pulled him away from the distraction. Within a minute, he had forgotten about the scent and was back to leading the way on our journey home.

The words I spoke to Archie were echoing in my ears… "You're just gonna have to forget about that." Sometimes God has to tell you and me the same thing. We get distracted on our pathway and get sidetracked by things that are either "none of our business" or are cleverly devised detours that the devil has set up to keep us from our destiny. There are even times that I've seen things in the morning news that stir up anger and frustration within me. I get distracted from my pathway (just like Archie) and God has to pull me back to my destiny and purpose with the words, "You're just gonna have to forget about that!"

Not everything you see, smell, feel and experience are healthy to your spiritual and mental well-being. Distractions and detours are everywhere. You can't get to the place God wants you to go if you're continually getting pulled away from His path. It is a wise person who can learn to say to himself, "You're just gonna have to forget about that!"

Philippians 3:13-14 (NAS)
Brethren, I do not regard myself as having laid hold of it yet; but one thing I do: forgetting what lies behind and reaching forward to what lies ahead, I press on toward the goal for the prize of the upward call of God in Christ Jesus.

TODAY'S WISDOM NUGGET
Concerning Temptation: If you can see and smell the forbidden fruit, you're hanging around too close to the tree.

"IF YOU ARE…."
March 5 | September 2

When Satan tempted Jesus in the wilderness, two of the three temptations started with the phrase "IF YOU ARE the Son of God…." This is a key phrase to remember. It is part of Satan's mode of operation to get a person to doubt their identity and relationship with God. After Jesus defeated the devil during the wilderness temptation Luke 4:13 says, "When the devil had finished all this tempting, he left him until an opportune time." Take note of that phrase "until an opportune time." You see, the wilderness was not the only time that Satan tried to tempt Jesus. Satan waited for an "opportune time." He waited for an OPPORTUNITY.

Now, think ahead, to when Jesus was dying on the cross. Do you remember what the Pharisees shouted to Jesus while he was dying on the cross? The tempter's voice was upon their lips as they said, "IF YOU ARE the Son of God come down from the cross" (Matthew 27:40). Satan had found an opportune time to once again tempt Jesus concerning His identity and relationship with God. Had Jesus given in to the temptation to prove Himself to the devil, you and I would be damned to an eternity in Hell, because our eternal destiny was hanging in the balance as Jesus obeyed the Father's wishes to redeem mankind through His sacrifice.

Jesus did not cave in to that temptation, but it is interesting to note that Satan tried once more to tempt Jesus while He was being crucified, as the thief hanging on the cross beside Him said "IF YOU ARE the Christ save yourself and us." (Luke 23:39)

Can you hear the tempter's voice whispering in your ear? He's not always just tempting you to sin. He also tempts you to doubt your true identity in God. Don't fall prey to this temptation. Find out what the Bible says about your identity "IN CHRIST" and stand firm in those words.

2 Corinthians 5:17
"If any man be IN CHRIST he is a new creature."

YOUR SMILE FOR THE DAY
Those who are well "grounded" will not be easily "shocked."
"…continue in the faith grounded and settled, and be not moved away from the hope of the gospel, which ye have heard." Colossians 1:23

THE GREATEST THING YOUR LEGS WILL DO
March 6 | September 3

Tim Steele was a close friend of mine for many years. Tim was no different from my other friends, except for one thing... he had spent all of his life in a wheelchair due to Cerebral Palsy. As a child, Tim had been told that he would most likely die by the age of 20 due to the disease that had crippled him. He was determined to live to 40 just to prove the doctors wrong. That's the kind of spirit he had, and he followed through with it.

At the age of 40, as the final days of his life were coming to an end, a small group of friends gathered around his bedside. We all knew that it was only a matter of days or weeks before he would "breathe his last breath." He had held on to the belief that he would be able one day to get up out of his wheelchair. That belief was to soon be fully realized in Heaven.

As we surrounded his bed, someone asked him, "What's the first thing you're going to do when you get to Heaven?" I suppose we all thought his response would be something like, "I'm going to RUN down the streets of gold on my new legs!" His quick reply to the question, though, caught us all by surprise when he said, "I'm going to find Jesus and bow down on my brand new knees and worship Him!" He continued, "All my life I've been in this wheelchair and haven't been able to worship my Lord by kneeling before Him... that's the first thing I want to do when I get to Heaven."

Tim taught us all an important lesson that day. The greatest thing a person will ever do with the legs that God has given them is not to stand, walk, run or play... it's to BOW BEFORE GOD ON BENDED KNEES. My brother, Tim, went on to Heaven several days later and I often think of the words of wisdom he passed on to us that day as we stood around his bedside. I know he is enjoying his brand new legs in Heaven... as He bows on his brand new knees before God's Throne.

Psalm 95:6
Come, let us bow down in worship, let us kneel before the LORD our Maker;

TODAY'S WISDOM NUGGET

Some people say, "Don't burn any bridges behind you." But I say, "Don't build your bridges out of materials that can be burned."

24
March 7 | September 4

In the Old Testament we read the story of the 12 tribes of Israel. In the New Testament we read the story of the 12 Apostles of Jesus Christ. 12+12=24. In the Book of Revelation we read about the 24 elders who are seated on thrones in Heaven (around God's throne), each with crowns of gold on their heads. In Revelation 4:10 we read that these 24 elders fall down before Him who sits on The Throne and they worship Him as they cast their crowns at His feet.

Now, if a person only receives the Old Testament as truth, he only has one set of 12... half of 24. And, if a person only receives the New Testament as truth, he only has one set of12 as well... only half of the story. If you receive both, however, you have a complete 24!

Now, here is where it gets rich, for there are 24 hours in a day, and we all want to experience all that each day offers... not just 12 of the available hours. A day is not COMPLETE until 24 hours have been experienced. I don't believe that it's just a coincidence that 24 elders are enthroned in Heaven. The 24 hours in our day need to be enthroned in Heaven as well, and each hour is so very valuable, like a crown of gold, and must be laid at the Master's feet to give Him proper worship.

Friend, we've been given 24 hours... two 12s. We should not discount one of the 12s because it is OLD, nor should we discount the other because it is NEW. We need the 12 hours of morning as well as the 12 hours of evening to make our day complete. Yes, it takes two 12s to make 24! You've been given 24 hours. Each and every single one is valuable, but its truest value is discovered when it is laid at Jesus' feet. Enjoy the 24 that you've been given!

Revelation 4:10 (NIV)
The twenty-four elders fall down before him who sits on the throne and worship him who lives for ever and ever. They lay their crowns before the throne....

TODAY'S FOOD FOR THOUGHT
God didn't call me to be a judge...
but I am a pretty decent fruit inspector!
Every tree is known by his own fruit - Luke 6:44

CALL IT THE WAY YOU SEE IT?
March 8 | September 5

I've heard people brag about their ability to be REALISTIC by saying, "I just call things the way I see them." Now, why would somebody brag about something like that? It takes no special ability, insight or talent to "call things the way you see them." It takes no creativity, no imagination, no effort and, most importantly, no faith. Even a toddler or preschooler can see a situation and repeat back to you exactly what they are seeing! "Calling things the way you see them" is very easy to do. Anybody can do it... so there's no need to boast in that ability. But, if you can see a situation that looks bleak and dark, possibly even hopeless, and you can speak a word of hope or positivity, you're doing something very special. It takes imagination, creativity, and, most importantly, it takes faith.

I think about God creating the world on the very first day of His creation. The Bible tells us that after He created the world that it was "empty and void, and darkness ruled over the face of the deep." Sounds pretty bleak to me! But God didn't "call things the way He saw them." No! Instead, He spoke what He wanted to exist, in spite of what was visually apparent to Him. He said, "LET THERE BE LIGHT!" The darkness was then overtaken by light because He refused to call things the way He saw them.

This is the heritage of the children of God. They don't "see things the way they are" so they don't "call things the way they are." They are like their Father in Heaven... the One who spoke LIGHT when all He saw was DARKNESS.

Romans 4:17
...God, who quickeneth the dead, and calleth those things which be not as though they were.

TODAY'S FOOD FOR THOUGHT
Have you ever thought about how strong and mighty God is? Jesus said that he cast out demons by the FINGER OF GOD (Luke 11:20). Imagine that... with one finger God can overpower a demon. Imagine what He could do with a FIST! And if you think His fist is powerful what do you suppose God could do if He "bared His Holy ARM?" (Isaiah 52:10). Do you have some demons pestering you? Others may not lift a finger to help you... but God will!

STAY CLOSE
March 9 | September 6

Almost every morning, I take my dog Archie with me on my morning walk to the local cemetery. It's a nice peaceful place for my morning quiet time. When we enter the gated area, I release Archie from his leash so he can move about freely. He enjoys the time of being "untethered" so he can run and play and roll around in the grass, sans leash.

There are times, however, when he gets too far away from me as he's enjoying that freedom and I have to remind him that he needs to STAY CLOSE. Close, where I can keep an eye on him… Close, where I can help him if he needs me… Close, where he stays safe from other animals that might be lurking about. So, those times when he strays too far away from me I will hide behind a tree, bush or garbage can in hopes that he will realize that he's "left my presence" and needs to return. It works every single time! When he recognizes the fact that his master isn't with him any longer he returns back in my direction to search for me.

Friends, I've heard people say things like, "God seems so far away" or "God seems so distant" and I can't help but wonder if they, just like Archie, went off doing their own thing, leaving God in a trail of smoke. Suddenly, they realize they're on their own and the Master is no where in sight. That feeling of missing His Presence is supposed to draw us back to Him, not to make us feel depressed and lonely. Yes, sometimes it seems like God is "hiding" from us, but if we'll examine the situation closely, we're the ones who have left Him, and He's just waiting on us to realize it so we can return to His side... so we can be safe in His Presence… so we will always remember to STAY CLOSE.

Jeremiah 29:13 (NAS)
You will seek Me and find Me when you search for Me with all your heart.

TODAY'S FOOD FOR THOUGHT
DEBT: something that is OWED to another.
"Forgive us our DEBTS as we forgive our debtors." Matthew 6:12
Put in other words: "Forgive us what we owe You in the same way we forgive others what they owe us". If you say that someone OWES you an apology or OWES you an explanation then they are INDEBTED to you... and more than likely you haven't forgiven them yet.

AMOUNTS VS. PERCENTAGES
March 10 | September 7

Bill Gate's net worth is reportedly 81 billion dollars. That's a whole lot of money. If he decided to give you just 1/1000th of one percent of his net worth you would have $810,000 dollars… you'd almost be a millionaire. If I, on the other hand, decided to give you 1/1000th of one percent of MY net worth you would have about $4… you could go buy a Happy Meal at McDonald's.

This makes me truly thankful that God is more interested in "percentages" than with "amounts." How do I know this? Well, one day Jesus was watching the rich people put their money in the temple treasury. They were giving huge amounts of money! But the person that captured his attention was a little widow woman who gave only two mites (just a half-penny). Jesus said that she put more into the treasury than all the others because they gave "out of their wealth" a small percentage of what they had, but she gave "everything she had" (100%).

People notice and appreciate amounts more than percentages, unfortunately. If Bill Gates put $810,000 in the church offering plate people would most likely stand in awe or applaud. The local newspaper would report on it, and it would probably make the evening news. But, to God, it would be no different than me putting $4 into the offering plate.

So, take heart today… God sees what you are giving and contributing. He's not impressed by large "amounts"… He's impressed by large "percentages"… He's impressed by those who "give their all."

Luke 21:3-4 (NIV)
"this poor widow has put in more than all the others. All these people gave their gifts out of their wealth; but she out of her poverty put in all she had to live on."

TODAY'S FOOD FOR THOUGHT
You can add a little lie to the truth and it becomes a lie, but if you add a little truth to a lie it remains a lie. Truth can have no additives. It must remain pure to remain true. Jesus said, "The truth will set you free," so if you're not experiencing freedom in your life, you should inspect the truth that you say you believe. Perhaps it's been tainted… with a lie.

A THIEF CALLED WORRY
March 11 | September 8

Have you ever left your house and your spouse says, "Did you remember to turn off the stove" and you reply, "Yes." But, then they say, "Are you SURE you turned off the stove?" So, you begin to think back, and you can't actually see a picture in your mind of yourself turning the stove off. All of a sudden, you're just a little unsure of yourself… not quite as confident as you were at the start. This is the great power that WORRY has. It steals your confidence in things you were once certain of. You return home, go to the kitchen and look at the stove and, sure enough, it is turned off just like you thought it was.

There are some people who understand that worry is not a good thing to have in their life, but they don't think it harms anyone else. The truth is, when you voice your worry for others to hear you might actually be harming them by stealing away their confidence. WORRY is a thief! It not only steals your confidence and trust in God, it could very well harm the confidence of others if it is allowed to speak.

Philippians 4:6 tells us how to defeat the Worry Thief when it says, "Don't worry about anything; instead, pray about everything. Tell God what you need, and thank him for all he has done." Don't let Worry steal from you and the others around you… defeat it with PRAYER!

My Confession for Today:
I will not let worry steal from me, or from the people who are in my life. I refuse to give worry a voice, for I know when it speaks it robs me of my confidence of God, and it also steals the confidence of those who listen to it coming from my lips. Worry is a thief. It is my enemy. I will not surrender my mouth to it! In Jesus' Name!

Luke 12:25-26 (NIV)
Who of you by worrying can add a single hour to your life ? Since you cannot do this very little thing, why do you worry about the rest?

TODAY'S WISDOM NUGGET
God has put some things in your hands and some in your heart. Your mission on earth is to let go of what He put in your hands and to hang on to what He put in your heart. The worst mistake a human can make is to get that turned around.

FOR THOSE WHO HAVE "NO ONE"
March 12 | September 9

In John chapter 5 we read about the Pool of Bethesda where miraculous healings took place. There were dozens (perhaps even hundreds) of sick and afflicted people who sat around the pool waiting for the waters to be stirred by an angel of God. As the story goes, the first person to enter the pool after the stirring of the water would be healed of their disease. Jesus met a man there who had been lame for 38 years and had hoped to be healed of his affliction as the waters were stirred. Unfortunately, because he was lame, he was not able to move quickly enough to reach the water in time as the waters were stirred. Someone always got ahead of him, and he had NO ONE to help him. Imagine that. The answer to your problem is just a few feet away, but you can't get to it, and NO ONE will help you get to it.

Jesus passed by dozens of other sick and afflicted people on that day and healed this one man. It is not recorded that Jesus healed any of the others at the Pool of Bethesda that day. I've often wrestled with this story, knowing that Jesus could have just as easily healed all of the sick and infirmed there, yet chose to heal just this one man. I don't understand all of the reasons behind this, but there are two very encouraging realities that we are left with:

1. Jesus is interested in helping individuals, not just multitudes. Wasn't it He who said that the shepherd will leave the ninety-nine sheep who are safe to go out and find THE ONE that is lost? Yes, God so loves "the world"… but He also loves "you."

2. Jesus is known for offering help to those who have NO ONE else. When Jesus is "all that you have" you are in for a blessing for sure!

So, be encouraged today by these truths. Jesus loves YOU as an individual, and will make you feel like you're the only one in the room even though you're surrounded by a multitude. He will pass by dozens and even hundreds of others who have help from other sources so He can get to someone who has NO ONE.

Psalm 142:4 (NIV)
Look and see, there is NO ONE at my right hand; NO ONE is concerned for me. I have no refuge; NO ONE cares for my life.

SIN
March 13 | September 10

Have you ever wondered how God decided what would be called "sin?" Did He just randomly pick certain vices and human tendencies and label them as sin for no particular reason? I mean, why is adultery and lying a sin, but singing in the shower is not? (Even though in some cases it should be.)

To answer this question let's go to the local pool. When we enter the gates of the pool we will see a list of Pool Rules. The rules are in place to keep us safe and protected from harm... harm that we might cause ourselves, or others. Why do the rules say that I can't dive into the shallow end of the pool? Because I could break my neck from such foolishness. The rule (law) protects me from the consequences of wrong actions (sins). Why can't I run around the pool? Because I could slip and fall and hurt myself, or even an innocent bystander. That's why that rule is in place.

God didn't come up with a list of sins to avoid so He could keep us from having fun or enjoying ourselves. He did it to protect us, and the others around us... people that He loves... people that He wants to bless with a long, healthy life. That blessing can be cut short if sin is not avoided.

There seems to be a lot of confusion these days about what sin is. Some are suggesting that things that once were considered sins years ago are no longer sins today because "we've advanced beyond that now." That's like saying, "It's okay to dive in the shallow end of the pool now... in the olden days it might have been wrong, but people can't break their necks doing that anymore." Crazy!

So, I'll just stick with the Bible on this. If the Bible calls it a sin I will do my best to avoid it, and if I participate in it I will quickly repent so that harm doesn't come to me... the harm that God was trying to protect me from by telling me to avoid the sin in the first place.

Romans 6:23
For the wages of sin is death, but the gift of God is eternal life through Christ Jesus our Lord.

TODAY'S WISDOM NUGGET
Part of your mission in life is to help other people discover their mission in life.

FULFILLING OUR PURPOSE
March 14 | September 11

Why did God create us? In Revelation 4:11 it says, "Thou art worthy, O Lord, to receive glory and honour and power: for thou hast created all things, and for THY PLEASURE they are and were created." So, let's ask that question again. Why did God create us? For His PLEASURE! Therefore, if God's specific purpose for our creation is to bring Him PLEASURE then no man will feel completely satisfied or fulfilled in life until he has PLEASED GOD.

Let me illustrate. We have a wooden spoon at our house. It was created to be a kitchen utensil, to stir food products during food preparation. Know what we're using it for? It is being used to prop open a window in our dining room! Even though it is fulfilling "a" purpose, it is not fulfilling "the" purpose it was specifically created for. I bet if that spoon could talk it would say, "I feel like something is missing in my life!" Ha!

You and I were created for a specific purpose. There are many things we do in this life that appear to be useful and fulfilling, but, until we tap into the specific purpose God created us for we will always feel like something is off… like something is missing. Our purpose is plain and simple: TO BRING GOD PLEASURE.

Now, just one final word on this. Hebrews 11:6 says "without FAITH it is impossible to please God." So, if we put all of this information together we find out that our purpose on Earth is to please God, and, since it's impossible to please Him without Faith, ultimately our purpose on Earth is to LIVE BY FAITH.

Friends, we must HAVE FAITH IN GOD… it will give us a sense of fulfillment and purpose like nothing else on Earth can.

Psalm 149:4
For the LORD taketh PLEASURE in his people: he will beautify the meek with salvation.

TODAY'S WISDOM NUGGET
To find the "bad guys," detectives look for fingerprints at the crime scene. We can do the same in our lives. Jesus said "the thief comes to STEAL, KILL and DESTROY"… those are his fingerprints. Never accuse God of doing something that has the devil's fingerprints on it.

SHAKEN
March 15 | September 12

After the major earthquakes in Nepal in 2015, I was thinking about the tremendous impact earthquakes have. I recalled something a friend of mine who had been in an earthquake told me. She said, "The worst thing about an earthquake is that feeling that the earth beneath your feet, that has supported you and that you've put so much trust in throughout your life, no longer feels reliable or dependable." What an incredible thought! If this earth can be shaken, and you can no longer have faith in its ability to hold you up safely and securely, where else can you put your faith for security and safety? When the thing you're standing on fails you, it's time to find a new foundation for your life.

God will let every false foundation in your life fail until you get to the place where you put your complete trust in Him. HE CANNOT BE SHAKEN. He is the most reliable foundation on which to build your life. If any of your "life's foundation" has failed you in recent weeks and months, it's quite possible that you're going through a time of SHAKING. When you're firmly standing on no other foundation except Jesus, the shaking process is completed.

My Prayer for Today:
"Lord, shake me! Shake the things out of my life that pretend to be my security and a firm foundation beneath my feet, but have no ability to hold me up in my times of crisis. You alone are my foundation!"

Hebrews 12:26-28 (NIV)
At that time his voice shook the earth, but now he has promised, "Once more I will shake not only the earth but also the heavens." The words "once more" indicate the removing of what can be shaken--that is, created things--so that what cannot be shaken may remain. Therefore, since we are receiving a kingdom that CANNOT BE SHAKEN, let us be thankful, and so worship God acceptably with reverence and awe

TODAY'S FOOD FOR THOUGHT
Today, I am who I am right now. Tomorrow, I'll be who I'm becoming. If you don't like me today, check back with me tomorrow!
"But we all, with unveiled face beholding as in a mirror the glory of the Lord, are being transformed into the same image from glory to glory."
2 Corinthians 3:18... HE'S CHANGING ME!

DISTRACTION = DESTRUCTION
March 16 | September 13

I was on my drive home from a neighboring town one Saturday after-noon, driving down the same country roads that I've driven down doz-ens of times before. I glanced over to my right and noticed some houses through the woods that I had never seen before. I thought to myself, "How could I have never noticed those houses before, after all the times I've passed them on this road?" As I looked back to the road I was driv-ing on I realized that I was about to run off the side of the road from the distraction. Ah, yes! That's why I had never noticed them before... because I was focused on the road ahead of me.

There is a road I'm traveling on in my life. That road leads me on my journey. There is a destination before me and hundreds (even thousands) of distractions along the way. I have to be careful about those distractions because if they capture my attention for too long, they can detour me or detain me in my journey. When I take my eyes off the road before me the smallest DISTRACTION could actually lead to my DESTRUCTION.

There is a name for the road that I am traveling on. Jesus called it the NARROW WAY. The alternative is the BROAD WAY. There's a lot more room for detours and distractions when you're on a BROAD road, but you've got to remind yourself that the BROAD WAY LEADS TO DE-STRUCTION.

So, I will continue to stay focused on the road ahead of me... the narrow road that Jesus has called me to. I have my eyes on the destination before me. Any distraction that pulls at me will only get a passing glance, as I remember these words of Jesus...

"Enter through the narrow gate. For wide is the gate and broad is the road that leads to DESTRUCTION, and many enter through it."
Matthew 7:13 (NIV)

TODAY'S FOOD FOR THOUGHT
Have you ever watched one of those cop shows where they have to disarm a bomb by gently clipping a couple of wires? They don't use hedge clippers and a jackhammer to do it. Got any potentially explosive situations you're dealing with? Be reminded of this verse:
"A GENTLE answer turns away wrath." Proverbs 15:1 NIV

THE POWER OF THE TONGUE
March 17 | September 14

Jesus told the disciples, "Wait in Jerusalem until you receive POWER from Heaven," so they waited, not knowing what the POWER would look like. Perhaps some of them wondered how this POWER would be manifested. Would it be a miracle-working POWER manifested through their hands? Would it be a mind-altering POWER manifested through their brains and minds?

There are a thousand and one ways that God could have demonstrated the power of His Holy Spirit through His disciples. He chose to do it, however, in a way that seems rather strange. The sound of a rushing mighty wind blew through that upper room, cloven tongues of fire appeared above their heads and the POWER was manifested through the disciples TONGUES.

No matter what your belief might be about Acts Chapter 2, the baptism of the Holy Spirit, and speaking in tongues, I think there is one thing that we all can agree upon: GOD WANTS OUR TONGUE! Our tongues (the words they speak) get us in more trouble than all of life's other vices combined. As a matter of fact, James 3:2 says, "For if we could control our tongues, we would be perfect and could also control ourselves in every other way." How can you tell if God really has a hold of a man? It's simple… just listen to his mouth… his tongue will reveal it.

Proverbs 18:21 says "Death and Life are in the POWER OF THE TONGUE." You can't go around speaking DEATH over yourself, your community and your world, and then try to convince me that you have the power of the Holy Spirit... Your tongue is working against you.

If you want power in life, the power that God gives will be manifested and experienced in your tongue. Your tongue will bring life to a dying world and to dying souls.

My Prayer for Today: "Lord, fill me with Your power… I surrender my TONGUE to your Holy Spirit."

TODAY'S FOOD FOR THOUGHT
The only hindrance to your full potential being reached is your own self-imposed limitations!
Greater is He that is in you, than he that is in the world. 1 John 4:4.

OVERCOMING PAIN
March 18 | September 15

I was talking to the guys at the Men's Home about the "pain in life" that we all experience, both physical and mental. I told them that none of us will make it through life without experiencing some kind of pain. How we handle the pain will be a big determining factor in the outcome of our lives. Then, from out of nowhere, I said some things that surprised me. The Holy Spirit rose up in me as I said, "That's the biggest issue I have with the use of drugs... people take them to numb themselves to their pain." (I'm saying this to a group of men who are sacrificing a year of their life to try to beat their drug addiction at this Men's Home.)

These words started flowing out of me before I even realized what I was saying. "No one wants to feel inner pain. If you have a choice between feeling good or experiencing pain, you'll choose "feeling good" every time. So, when you take drugs to mask your pain, or numb yourself to your pain, you are in no position to overcome your pain. Thus, you will have to deal with it again and again throughout your life, because you never conquered it." When Jesus was dying on the cross, experiencing pain both in body and soul that none of us have ever come close to experiencing, He cried out, "I Thirst!" The scripture says that he was offered a drink of "wine mixed with myrrh." This mixture had medicinal value, bringing a numbing sensation to those who drank it, numbing them to the pain that they were experiencing. Jesus refused the drink. He refused the opportunity to become numb to His pain. After all, part of His sacrifice on the cross was for him to experience our pain... and to take it away.

The pains of life are not fun at all. We have 3 options in handling the pain in our lives: 1) Succumb, 2) Grow Numb, or, 3) Overcome. In Revelation 2 and 3 Jesus tells us the rewards that He has prepared for "him who overcomes." To experience His blessing when we're dealing with "inner pain" we must not SUCCUMB, or GROW NUMB... we must OVERCOME!

Rev. 2:7
To him who overcomes, I will grant to eat of the tree of life which is in the Paradise of God.'

TODAY'S FOOD FOR THOUGHT
Lord, PROTECT us from the influence and illusion of
"the temporary" and CONNECT us to the reality of "the eternal."

LOVING THE FATHER
March 19 | September 16

I was sitting at my computer desk, working on an important deadline one day when, from out of nowhere, my teenage son came up behind me and hugged me around my neck. Supposing that to be his way of telling me he needed something from me, I said, "What was that for?" But, he simply replied, "Just because." When I realized that he was sincere, that he just wanted to do it because he loved me, I stopped what I was doing and said, "I'm taking you to lunch! Where do you want to go?" His release of affection towards me stirred me to do something to reciprocate.

Receiving unexpected (and unrequested) affection from your child is an awesome thing. Sometimes, we get so accustomed to our children coming to us with all their needs that we forget they have something to offer us as well. What a blessing just to have your child "love on you!"

Now, I'm sure God delights in the fact that we come to Him with all of our needs. He's such a Good Father. Imagine, though, how much it must bless Him when we come to Him, without a single prayer request or need, and simply tell Him that we Love Him and Worship Him. If a father like me, riddled with faults and imperfections, can be blessed and moved to action by the affection of one of my children, HOW MUCH MORE is Father God moved by the expressions of affection and praise from one of His children?

Today, I'd like to suggest that, instead of always going to Father God with your list of wants and needs, that you occasionally go to Him with a simple heart of thanks and gratitude, and just let Him know that you love Him. You might be pleasantly surprised by His response!

Matthew 7:11 (NAS)
"If you then, being evil, know how to give good gifts to your children, HOW MUCH MORE will your Father who is in heaven give what is good to those who ask Him!" [Words of Jesus]

PUT YOUR THINKING CAP ON

The LORD JEHOVAH is my strength and my song; he also is become my salvation - Isaiah 12:2. He is my Strength, my Song and my Salvation. He's my Shepherd, my Source and Supply, my Sanctuary, my Stronghold. Are there any other "S" words that describe God?

UPON HIS SHOULDER
March 20 | September 17

I woke up one morning with an interesting Bible verse resonating in my mind and heart: "The government shall be upon His shoulder." (Isaiah 9:6, a prophetic verse foretelling of the coming of the Messiah)

The phrase "upon His shoulder" insinuates that Jesus will carry the weight of government (in my opinion, both earthly and heavenly). Whatever other meaning there might be in that verse I know this: If Jesus is carrying the weight of something on His shoulders, then it is a weight that I'm not supposed to carry. He carries the weight for me.

The scripture tells us that we are to cast all of our cares upon Jesus (1 Peter 5:7). There are cares that we are not meant to carry. They weigh us down and steal our peace and joy. Hebrews 12:1 tells us to "lay aside every weight... and let us run with patience the race that is set before us." You can't run a race effectively when you are carrying unnecessary weight. Jesus criticized the Pharisees of His day when He said, "They bind heavy burdens, hard to bear, and lay them on men's shoulders" (Matthew 23:4). The devil would like nothing more than to "weigh us down" with unnecessary burdens so that our lives become ineffective for God.

The government, the weight and burden of it, is upon Jesus shoulders... so it should not be upon mine.

My Prayer for Today:
"Father forgive me for taking on a burden in this life that I was not meant to carry. I cast my cares and concerns about government and politics upon you. I will run my race without carrying this burden... and thus, I will finish stronger, with more stamina, and with greater results."

Psalm 55:22 (NIV)
Cast your cares on the LORD and he will sustain you; he will never let the righteous be shaken.

TODAY'S FOOD FOR THOUGHT
People who wait on the Lord get their strength renewed. And not just ordinary strength to walk or run. No, they receive a special strength to do something incredible... they receive strength to FLY. *"They shall mount up with winds as eagles"* - Isaiah 40:31

WHERE'S THE FLAVOR?

March 21 | September 18

Have you ever had a cold or a sinus infection that was so bad that you couldn't taste any of the food you were eating? I remember one time I was eating a nice, big, juicy $12 hamburger at a restaurant, but I had a sinus infection and I couldn't taste anything. It might as well have been a cheap bowl of oatmeal. I felt like I wasted my money. Yes, my belly was full, but my taste-buds weren't satisfied. Most of the enjoyment of eating comes from TASTING.

Sometimes life is like that. All the good things in life seem to have lost their "taste" and we just go through the motions. Eat…chew… swallow… belly is full, but there was no taste, and thus, no enjoyment. JOY is to LIFE what TASTE is to EATING. Sure, you can LIVE without experiencing JOY, just like you can EAT without TASTING. Your belly can be satisfied while your taste-buds are dissatisfied. But the pleasure in eating comes from tasting… and the pleasure in living comes from enjoying.

In John 15:11, Jesus said "I have told you this so that my joy may be in you and that your joy may be complete." Jesus didn't die for us just so we could "live." He died for us that we might have "joy." He paid the price for us to have joy! Ask God to open your eyes to the joy in life that you've been missing. Joy is the FLAVOR OF THE SAVIOR!

My Prayer for Today: "Lord, help me to experience the joy that you died to give me. Life has flavor when joy is present in my life. I don't want to live another day where joy is absent. Help me to focus on the good and positive things in life that boost my joy level. And, as I overflow with Your joy inside me, may it spill over on those around me who desperately need to "Taste and See" that the Lord is Good!"

Psalm 34:8 (NIV)
Taste and see that the LORD is good; blessed is the man who takes refuge in him.

TODAY'S FOOD FOR THOUGHT

God doesn't underestimate the value of ONE... neither should we.
"What man of you, having an hundred sheep, if he lose one of them, doth not leave the ninety and nine in the wilderness, and go after that which is lost, until he find it?" Luke 15:4

STUCK!
March 22 | September 19

An embarrassing thing happened to me after church one wet Sunday morning. I drove my truck into a muddy area, not realizing that the ground was completely saturated from all the recent rain. You guessed it! I got my truck stuck in the mud. I couldn't move forwards or backwards. It's a pretty helpless feeling when you're stuck like that and you realize that it was your own ignorance that got you there!

A friend drove by and I asked if he could help pull me out with his truck. But, there wasn't enough dry ground nearby where he could get the traction he needed to pull me out and I only had an 8' chain to pull with. If he had tried to pull me out he would have gotten stuck too. We found a guy with a bigger, 4-wheel drive truck who had a 20' chain and he got up on the main road, with his chain connected to my trailer hitch, and he easily pulled me out to solid ground. I had been rescued from my embarrassing moment. Lesson learned? You've got to be on solid ground if you're going to help somebody who's stuck in the mire!

It's embarrassing in life when you get stuck, especially when you know it's your own fault. People in this world are stuck in the mire of sin and shame, and they need help. But, the truth is, we can't help somebody who's "stuck" by getting in the mud with them… we've got to be on solid ground. Sure, we want to show empathy and compassion by getting down on the level where they are. But, they are not helped if we get STUCK with them.

God, and His Word, are the most stable and reliable foundations that a person can have in this life. To reject the strength offered from His firm foundation is to succumb to a life of being STUCK. People who stand on His foundation are not any better than those who are stuck in the mire of sin, but they are in a better location. They've moved to a place of stability and strength, and have a firm foundation beneath their feet.

It's embarrassing to be stuck in the mire of sin, but it's more embarrassing to stay stuck when a life of freedom is just inches away. To get unstuck you'll need help from somebody who is on Solid Ground. On Christ the Solid Rock I stand… all other ground is sinking sand!

Psalm 40:2
He brought me up also out of an horrible pit, out of the miry clay, and set my feet upon a rock, and established my goings.

OUR SPIRITUAL UMBILICAL CORD

March 23 | September 20

While we were still in our mother's womb we were connected to her by means of an umbilical cord. That connection was our "life source" and without it we would not have survived. When we were born that cord was cut... our life source and supply would now be dependent on what the Earth could supply. So we spend many years of our early lives trying to connect to the things of the Earth to fill our needs and desires. But, because the Earth is cursed, though we are filled by it we still remain empty because our new life source is imperfect and corrupt. This can lead a person to depression, feelings of hopelessness and unhappiness.

However, when a person gets "born again" they get connected to the Kingdom of God by means of a spiritual umbilical cord. Their life source and supply now comes from a place of limitless abundance. No longer connected to the Earth for their supply or happiness, believers do not display the same concern over faltering economies and politics as those still tethered to the corrupt Earth system. Their source and supply remains unhindered no matter what happens in the Earth system. No wonder Jesus used these words in His prayer to the Father to describe His followers: "They are not of this world, even as I am not of this world." (John 17:16) When an unbeliever dies, still connected to the Earth as his source and supply, there is no life transferred from the Earth to his mortal flesh... he is truly, completely dead. But when a believer dies, still connected to Heaven's supply by means of that spiritual umbilical cord, he is resuscitated by that supply and transferred into Heaven's splendor without undergoing the pain and torment associated with death.

So, taking all of this into consideration, ask yourself today where your life source and supply comes from. Does it come from a faltering Earth system that can never fully satisfy? Or, are you connected to the unlimited supply provided through the "umbilical cord" of Heaven?

Philippians 4:19 (NAS) "God will supply all your needs"

TODAY'S FOOD FOR THOUGHT

On the day of His baptism, before Jesus had performed one single miracle, the heavens opened and the voice of God said, "This is my beloved son in whom I am well-pleased." So it is with us also. God is pleased, not by our performance FOR Him, but our relation TO Him.

A LESSON FROM TOILET PAPER
March 24 | September 21

Oddly enough, my Thought for Today comes directly from a package of toilet paper. While I was reading the front of the packaging I noticed that the word "Stronger" in English was translated as "Résistant" in French. Of course, I realize that it is not a literal translation of the word, but, still it gave me an even better appreciation for the word STRONGER. You see, we often associate STRENGTH with physical ability and capability. We say a person is getting STRONGER when they are putting on muscle mass and gaining exterior mobility and agility. But an even greater meaning of the word is discovered when we add the thought of RESISTANCE.

There are muscle-bound men and women who are not able to RESIST even the smallest of temptations that they face. They are STRONG on the outside but WEAK on the inside because they have no RESISTANCE. Yes, when a person possesses the ability to RESIST an urge or harmful desire, they show an inward STRENGTH that, in this world, is not greatly appreciated. When the Bible tells us to "BE STRONG in the Lord and in the power of His might" (Ephesians 6:10) it's not telling us to put on muscle mass. It's telling us to gain an inward strength by which we are able to RESIST our enemy. After all, Ephesians 6 is all about the armor of God and our battle against the enemy of our souls. There are frail little grandmothers, who are kneeling before God this day in prayer, who are ten times STRONGER than the Muscle-head working out at the local gym.

Are you STRONG today? And when I say STRONG I really mean RESISTANT. There's so much more to STRENGTH than what we fully understand… a package of toilet paper told me so!

1 Corinthians 16:13 (NAS)
Be on the alert, stand firm in the faith, act like men, be STRONG.

James 4:7 (NAS)
Submit therefore to God. RESIST the devil and he will flee from you.

TODAY'S FOOD FOR THOUGHT
The Israelites went through a wilderness… then they entered the Promised Land. Jesus went through a wilderness… then started his preaching and healing ministry. The wilderness may not be great, but what awaits on the other side of the widerness is!

PROBLEMS IN THE FAMILY
March 25 | September 22

Somebody recently told me of a Christian who became an atheist because he said the hypocrites in the church made him turn away from God. I shook my head in disbelief and replied, "That's like me saying to my wife 'I'm leaving you because I don't like the way our kids are acting!'" If Christianity is just an "Ideology," just a system of beliefs and values, then I can see how someone could leave the "system" due to the inconsistencies of others who supposedly embrace it. But Christianity is not an ideology... it is a living relationship with a loving Father. I am not denying that there are hypocrites out there, but I want to offer a different viewpoint to give you something to think about.

If you have a large family then you have many different ages and levels of maturity within that unit (just like in God's Family). There are newborns, who mess their diapers, throw up on themselves, and cry frequently. There are toddlers who are learning to walk, who stumble and fall, who make messes that we have to clean up. There are adolescents who are full of energy, growing rapidly and changing daily, trying to find their place. There are teenagers, who are truly young adults, but who still look like kids, who are discovering their independence while pushing our buttons and testing the boundaries. All of these age groups are part of "The Family."

You don't leave the Family when the baby messes his diapers, when the toddler drops his cup, when the adolescent's voice cracks, or when the teenager stays out past his curfew... that would be nonsense. We understand that they are not yet grown and mature, so we show them mercy, because we see that they are part of the FAMILY. If you are in GOD'S FAMILY the same thought applies. We are all at different levels of maturity in our relationship with Him. If you leave His family because a baby "messes his diapers" you don't understand what FAMILY means.... and you're acting like a 4-year-old who runs away from home when he doesn't get his way.

Christianity is a relationship with a Father and His family. Sure, some of His kids are stinkers, but I'm not severing my relationship with Him because of the immature behavior of one of His other kids... that would be pretty immature of me!

Ephesians 3:14-15 (NAS)
For this reason I bow my knees before the Father, from whom every family in heaven and on earth derives its name.

WHO IS THE GREATEST?
March 26 | September 23

I asked for two volunteers from my Elementary kids at church to help serve pizza to the other kids in the class. I was pleased to see so many of the kids raise their hands to help. I called on Ethan and Peter to serve and they did a great job asking each person what they wanted to eat and putting it on their plate for them. When they had served everyone in class I let them fix a plate for themselves.

Later on we went over our lesson and memory verse for the night. Our memory verse was "The Son of Man did not come to be served, but to serve, and to give His life as a ransom for many." (Mark 10:45) I told the children that Jesus said those who serve others are GREATEST in His kingdom. Then I asked them to imagine that a person from another country was peeking in the window while Ethan and Peter were serving the other kids. That person might conclude that Ethan and Peter were inferior to the other kids in the class since they were serving. I said, "In this world when you see someone serving somebody else the thought is that the person being served is superior to (or more important than) the one who is serving." But, then I asked them to imagine God looking down from Heaven as the two boys served the other kids, and I asked, "Who do you think God sees as being more important?" They answered correctly, "Ethan and Peter."

I want to do my part to raise up a new generation of kids who have God's mindset and His perspective. Kids who understand that greatness isn't achieved by "working your way to the top" and making a name for yourself, but by serving others and giving of self. To see all of the entitlement issues that our modern society struggles with makes me all the more eager to instill this idea in the next generation. Will you help the cause? If you have kids, or work with kids, would you please instill in them the importance of serving others? You want them to be "great" don't you?

Matthew 23:11
But he who is greatest among you shall be your servant.

TODAY'S FOOD FOR THOUGHT
When you have an unexplained desire to perform an act of kindness and then do it, you are responding to the voice of God in your life.

LORD, HEAL MY SOUL
March 27 | September 24

Psalm 41:4
I said, LORD, be merciful unto me: HEAL MY SOUL; for I have sinned against thee.

Some sins affect our flesh… some our soul. It's easy to see the ones that affect our flesh. It's not so easy to see the ones that affect our soul. The meth addict has rotten teeth, the alcoholic has a bad liver, the promiscuous person has STDs, etc., etc. But, what about the unforgiving, the envious and the bitter? Their sin does not affect them outwardly as much as inwardly. Their flesh may not need to be healed… but their soul does.

How sad it must be to be physically, outwardly whole yet inwardly broken and in need of repair. You can fool others, who can only see what is outwardly manifested in your life, but YOU are not fooled. You know your soul is not right. This is what David was most likely expressing when he wrote the above passage in the book of Psalms. David is also quoted as saying, "He restores my soul." (Psalm 23)

We are more than just physical beings. We have a soul… a soul that can be just as guilty of sin as our unbridled flesh… a soul that needs healing from time-to-time. Though all may seem okay with us outwardly, our souls can be diseased and afflicted. A good bit of soul searching would do us all good… followed by a good bit of "soul healing."

My Prayer for Today:
"Lord, forgive me of the sins I've committed that have affected my soul. Sins that have been covered up, that others can't see, but that I am aware of, and You are aware of. I repent of the sins in my soul and I know that as I repent of them that You forgive me and bring healing to my soul."

Psalm 139:23-24
Search me, O God, and know my heart: try me, and know my thoughts: And see if there be any wicked way in me.

TODAY'S FOOD FOR THOUGHT

1 Corinthians 3:9 says, "Don't give the devil a foothold." The verse right before that one talks about dealing with anger in our lives. Unresolved anger gives the devil a "foothold"… plain and simple.

GET "RIGHT" BY CONFESSING "WRONG"

March 28 | September 25

Proverbs 24:16 (NIV)
For though the righteous fall seven times, they rise again

No, I do not say that I never mess up. No, I do not believe that I'm perfect. No, I am not saying that I am better than anyone else. I am aware of my inconsistencies. I am aware of the wrong that I do. I am aware of my bad attitudes and poor judgment. I admit that I fall from time to time. I try my best to make quick adjustments and repent when I have done wrong. I don't hold on to the wrong and "own" it and claim it as part of who I am. I denounce it. It is an inconsistency in my life that is not in keeping with God's Word and His commands. As the above scripture states so plainly, even though I fall, I rise again. I don't stay down. I repent and "rise again" to right standing with God (the definition of "righteous.") I'm embarrassed to admit that I do wrong. It is not good for my reputation. I don't feel good about myself when I make this type of confession, but it is necessary for me to admit my WRONG if I want to get RIGHT.

This is why I'm so concerned about the world we live in. Particularly in the "politically correct" climate that now exists. No one is willing to admit that they're wrong. To confess that you are wrong is a humbling experience… it hurts your reputation… it lets others know that you are not "perfect." But, it is a necessary ingredient to being made RIGHT with God… confessing WRONG.

So, here's the difference between a righteous man and a wicked man: A righteous man falls, and he rises again. A wicked man falls, and won't admit that he has fallen and, thus, remains fallen. Friends, there is no shame in admitting that you fall, or that you have fallen. The shame is to be fallen but deny it, and pretend that you've "risen" while you're still laying flat on your back.

1 John 1:9
If we confess our sins He is faithful and just to forgive us our sins and to cleanse us from all unrighteousness.

TODAY'S FOOD FOR THOUGHT
To have salvation without any joy is like eating chocolate and not tasting it. Joy is the Flavor of the Savior.

HIDE AND SEEK
March 29 | September 26

When my kids were preschool age they liked for me to play "Hide and Seek" with them in our home. It was always a challenge for me to find a hiding place that could conceal all 6 feet 3 inches of my frame. One particular day I remember cleverly concealing myself behind a coat rack in the corner of the living room. My upper torso and head were covered by coats and jackets but my legs were completely uncovered. As I spied through the jackets I could see my kids walk by looking for me. They must have passed right by me a half dozen times. After having no luck in finding me they got distracted from the search and gave up. To pull them back into the game I let out a little yelp to get them focused back on the search. It was so cute to see their little faces light up when they finally found me.

It is a challenging quest that we are on, for those of us who call ourselves "Christians." God's Word encourages us with such passages as "seek the Lord while He may be found," and "You will seek Me and find me, when you search for me with all your heart" (Isaiah 55:6, Jeremiah 29:13). He does not conceal Himself totally from our view. He gives us helpful "hints" on how to find Him if we will pay attention. But, life brings so many distractions our way that we often give up the search and lose our focus. If we will listen closely though, we will hear His voice calling us back to the search. He knows what awaits us if we don't give up, for Hebrews 11:6 tells us that "He is a rewarder of those who seek him DILIGENTLY."

Don't give up "the quest!" Keep searching until you get the REWARD!

Matthew 7:7-8 (NIV)
Ask and it will be given to you; seek and you will find; knock and the door will be opened to you. For everyone who asks receives; he who seeks finds; and to him who knocks, the door will be opened.

Acts 17:27 (KJV)
That they should seek the Lord, if haply they might feel after him, and find him, though he be not far from every one of us.

YOUR SMILE FOR TODAY
The difference between a legalist and a hypocrite:
The legalist says "That looks like fun... it must be sin!"
The hypocrite says "That looks like sin... it must be fun!"

WHERE ALL OF OUR PROBLEMS BEGAN
March 30 | September 27

Where did all of our problems begin? We could go back to the garden of Eden where Adam and Eve disobeyed God and ate the forbidden fruit. Yes, we could say that DISOBEDIENCE is where all of our problems began. But, let's go back further than that, to before the fruit was eaten and a deceptive serpent lied to Eve about the truth of God's words. Yes, we could say that a LIE is where all of our problems began. But, let's go back even further than that, to a time before God created the world and there was a perfect Heaven… where one angel thought he deserved greater recognition… where one angel didn't like the fact that God was the constant focus… where one angel became filled with PRIDE and led a Heavenly revolt against the One who created him. Yes, PRIDE is where all of our problems began.

Lucifer's Pride disturbed the splendor and perfection of Heaven. God could not let Heaven's splendor be spoiled and disturbed. Pride had to be banished along with the root of that pride that was in Lucifer's heart.

Lucifer's Pride… God knows exactly what it looks like… He knows exactly what would happen again in Heaven if he let one ounce of it enter through the Pearly Gates. Heaven is not a place of competition. There will be no more Heavenly battles… God will see to it.

Because God loves us and wants us to be with Him in Heaven, He will do all He can to extract the smallest amount of Lucifer's Pride that is in us. We may not even realize how deadly our pride can be but God knows all too well the division and strife that pride can create within a totally peaceful and perfect environment. I've seen Lucifer's Pride in government, in the business world, in sporting events, in Hollywood and even in the church, but what bothers me the most is when I see it in the mirror. "Lord, extract pride from my life. Do your surgery on me. Remove it completely from my heart!"

1 Peter 5:6 (NAS)
Therefore humble yourselves under the mighty hand of God, that He may exalt you at the proper time.

TODAY'S FOOD FOR THOUGHT
Romans 8:31 asks the question, "If God be for us who can be against us?" The answer is not "No one". The answer is "It doesn't matter!"

THANKFUL FOR THE LITTLE THINGS
March 31 | September 28

The last 2 years of Tim Steele's life were spent on a feeding tube and a ventilator due to the debilitating disease Cerebral Palsy. Because of this Tim did not have a single drop of water, or any beverage of any kind, to come across his lips in those 2 years. One day while I was visiting with him he said to me with labored breath through his ventilator tube, "Greg, promise me something." I didn't know what I was getting myself into so I said, "Okay, if it's something that I can do, I promise I'll do it." He continued, "Promise me that before you drink your next glass of water you'll get down on your knees and thank God for giving you the opportunity to drink water." Wow! I had never even once thought about what a blessing it was to be able to drink a nice cold, refreshing glass of water until Tim had said that. So, I agreed to his request and when I got home that day I poured a nice cold glass of water for myself and got down on my knees in my kitchen floor, raised my hands toward Heaven, and thanked God for it.

Tim passed away a few months later. I still think of him often… especially when I'm drinking a glass of cold, refreshing water. I thank God for this simple little pleasure of life that I've been blessed with, all because someone reminded me what a blessing it is. Sometimes we don't even realize the things we should be thankful for until someone reminds us… until we see it from someone else's eyes.

My Prayer for Today: "Lord, show me the things that I take for granted in my life… the things I should be thankful for that I completely overlook. Teach me how to be thankful for even the smallest of this life's blessings.

1 Thessalonians 5:18
In everything give thanks; for this is God's will for you in Christ Jesus.

TODAY'S WORD OF ENCOURAGEMENT
In the beginning God used His HAND to form Adam. He then used His MOUTH to breathe into Adam and to speak His instructions. We are all just like Adam… we all need a touch from God's HAND and a word from His MOUTH. May you receive both today!
"We all are the work of thy HAND." Isaiah 64:8
"Man shall not live by bread alone, but by every word that proceedeth out of the MOUTH of God." Matthew 4:4

THE FIRST ORDER OF CREATION
April 1 | September 29

Have you discovered yet that God does things in sequence... in a progression. Just look to the front of the book He gave us and you'll see that He does things "in order." You need look no further than Genesis 1:3 to discover that LIGHT is the very first order of business with God. What good does it do to create beautiful waterfalls, colorful flowers and deep blue oceans if there is no LIGHT with which to see them? Yes, LIGHT is the very first thing that God created in the order of things.

In our lives, when He's creating in us, LIGHT is the very first order of creation as well. A man, whose soul and spirit are in darkness, will never see beauty in his life or in his surroundings until LIGHT has been shed on his situation. You've got to have LIGHT to be able to see. It's just that simple.

So, maybe we've been praying for our situations the wrong way. Maybe we should first pray that LIGHT will be shed on the situation so we can see it correctly. Maybe there are things we aren't seeing correctly simply because not enough LIGHT is available. Take a hint from Genesis 1:3... when you're praying for that situation, say "LET THERE BE LIGHT!"

My Prayer for Today: "Lord, shine Your light on the situations in my life. Darkness has hidden beauty and truth from me. But, Your light gives me the ability to see what is hidden... what has been cloaked in darkness. Let there be LIGHT in my life!"

John 8:12 (NIV)
When Jesus spoke again to the people, he said, "I am the light of the world. Whoever follows me will never walk in darkness, but will have the light of life."

Matthew 4:16 (KJV)
The people which sat in darkness saw great light; and to them which sat in the region and shadow of death light is sprung up.

TODAY'S FOOD FOR THOUGHT
Remember: SEEKers learn SEEKrets (Secrets)
Deuteronomy 29:29 "The SECRET things belong unto the LORD our God." Daniel 2:22 "He revealeth the deep and SECRET things." Hebrews 11:6 "He is a rewarder of them that diligently SEEK him."

THE TEMPERED STRENGTH OF GOD
April 2 | September 30

When my kids were preschool age I used to wrestle with them on our living room floor. Every once in a while I would "pin them" to the floor just to remind them that I was "the boss," but most of the time I would let them beat me so they could know the thrill of victory. Unknowingly, I gave them a mistaken idea of the amount of strength I had. One night, my wife and I went out and had a friend babysit our kids. Evidently they asked her if she would wrestle with them and she agreed to do so. My friend didn't know about my policy of letting the kids win so she wrestled with them for several minutes and always won each match. When the wrestling was over my son exclaimed to the babysitter, "Wow! You're stronger than my dad!"

Funny story, but it leads me to this point. Do we realize how much God tempers His strength so He can be with us?! We pray, "Lord, touch me" not realizing that His touch could very well crush us if not tempered. We say, "Lord, breathe on me" forgetting that the breath of His nostrils parted the waters of the Red Sea. We say, "Lord, show us Your glory" not fathoming the truth of the scripture "No man can see Me and live." We say, "Lord, fill my cup" not realizing that God has an ocean-sized basin from which to pour into our thimble-sized cup! No wonder David says "my cup overflows!" And perhaps this is the reason why God is called "More Than Enough, El Shaddai." It is not because He is wasteful... it is because His strength is so much greater than what we ask for or need that His cutoff valve can't be turned off quickly enough. Remember the feeding of the 5,000? 12 basketfuls of leftovers from 5 loaves of bread and two fish!

So the next time you're in God's presence, think of what a blessing it is to fellowship with your Father. As you enjoy His embrace, be careful not to say, "Hold me tighter, Lord!" HaHa!

Psalm 113:5-6 (NIV)
Who is like the LORD our God, Who is enthroned on high, Who humbles Himself to behold The things that are in heaven and in the earth?

TODAY'S WORD OF ENCOURAGEMENT
The Lord has promised to never forget you! Here's what He says:
"I will not forget you. Behold, I have inscribed you on the palms of My hands"- Isaiah 49:15-16. You're always on His mind. More importantly, the memory of you is always on the palms of His nail-scarred hands.

ENLARGE
April 3 | October 1

Many people got on the Prayer of Jabez "band wagon" several years ago. It's a great prayer! One point of emphasis in the prayer is the phrase "ENLARGE my borders" (1 Chronicles 4:10). Right after you pray that scripture, confess this one over yourself, "I shall run the way of Thy commandments, For Thou wilt ENLARGE my heart" (Psalm 119:32). Did you get that? ENLARGE my HEART. No doubt, in a medical sense an enlarged heart is not a good thing to have. But when it comes to matters of the soul and spirit it's imperative that believers have a "big heart!"

A missionary to Africa had come to America to a Leadership Conference. I don't know what her message was "supposed to be" but when she got on the platform and stood behind the podium in front of thousands of American church leaders she began to weep. She pointed to her head while weeping and said, "Too big!" Then she pointed to her heart, still weeping, and said ,"Too small!" She did this over and over again for several minutes. That was the entirety of the message. Many of the leaders in that room began to weep, along with the missionary, in repentance for allowing their minds to become so dominant in their ministries as their hearts had gotten smaller and colder. One man, however, left the auditorium in total anger, saying, "I came hundreds of miles to get information to help my ministry grow and all I get is a babbling woman talking nonsense!" As he got into his car in the parking deck and put the keys in the ignition the Lord spoke to his heart and told him, "That message was for YOU." When the reality hit him he began to weep in his car and prayed a prayer of repentance.

Jesus said that a sign of the end times will be that "the love of many will grow cold" (Matthew 24:12). As hearts grow cold they contract and become smaller, with less room for love to fill them. Purpose in your heart not to let that happen to you! Refuse to become a "sign of the end times."

My Prayer for Today: "Lord, Warm my heart today so that I don't become another "sign of the end times." Enlarge my heart!

TODAY'S WISDOM NUGGET
The difference between a flatterer and an encourager is this: A flatterer says something nice to you with the intended purpose that you will like THEM better. The encourager will say something nice to you with the intended purpose that you will like YOURSELF better.

TAKE A KID TO CHURCH
April 4 | October 2

You never know how great of an impact you can have in this life by following through and doing the simplest of things for others. Take, for instance, the case of the Whitten family.

When I was 13 years old my family lived next door to the Whitten family. My family didn't go to church but the Whittens went regularly. They invited me to go to their church and they offered me a ride. I enjoyed it and was shown a lot of love there so I wanted to go back. My parents didn't want to go but they didn't mind me going, so the Whittens were more than happy to bring me along... for 4 straight years! Every Sunday morning, Sunday night and Wednesday night! I didn't miss a single service in those 4 years thanks to caring neighbors. Oh, and did I mention, I got saved at a Wednesday night service that the Whittens brought me to? I'm a born-again believer in Jesus Christ with a future home in Heaven because the Whittens "offered me a ride to church!"

I have thought about the Whittens from time to time over the years and the great impact they have had in my life simply by giving me a ride to church. In more recent years I attended a fellowship supper at my church and sat down at a table to eat with a sweet sister in the Lord. We were talking about the 3 boys that I had brought to church with me that night and she said, "Thank you for bringing them to church with you. It reminds me of the story you tell about the neighbors who used to bring you to church!" And then the light came on! What the Whittens did for me I was now doing for others... the cycle continues. Their act of service to the Lord was a seed planted in me that had grown and matured, and now I was planting seeds in others. Taking a kid to church is a simple thing to do, but it could very well change their entire destiny. I know... it changed mine!

Matthew 25:40 (NIV)
...whatever you did for one of the least of these brothers and sisters of mine, you did for me.

TODAY'S WISDOM NUGGET
They say that your ATTITUDE will determine your ALTITUDE (how high you'll reach). Perhaps your GRATITUDE will determine your LATITUDE (how wide you'll reach). A grateful person with a good attitude has unlimited potential!

INSATIABLE DESIRE
April 5 | October 3

This is not meant to be a downer but the truth is: "Everything on Earth slowly loses its appeal." It is a hard, cold fact of life. Sociologists say that humans have something called INSATIABLE DESIRE, which basically means "it's impossible to satisfy them." From this term we get sayings like "the grass is always greener on the other side" and "the honeymoon is over." Everything that is NEW in our lives will undoubtedly one day either lose its luster or will be taken for granted. What someone else possesses will soon look more appealing to us than our own possessions. People have done hundreds of things to try to fill that INSATIABLE DESIRE: they've changed marriage partners, changed jobs and even changed religions.

You may be dealing with INSATIABLE DESIRE in your life right now. That feeling inside is one of the things that, if handled correctly, will lead you to one of life's most important revelations... YOU'RE NOT GOING TO LIVE HERE FOREVER! To be totally satisfied on an Earth that is cursed and destined for destruction could be very detrimental. This dissatisfaction in us reminds us "this is not all there is." Do you remember, in the Garden of Eden, why God sent Adam out of the garden? He did not want him to eat of the TREE OF LIFE "lest he stretch out his hand, and take also from the tree of life, and eat, and live forever" (Gen.3:22). What a terrible state Adam would have been in to live forever, totally and completely dissatisfied because of the effects of sin!

Thankfully there is greener grass for all of us, but it's not on this planet. It's on the other side.... in a place called Heaven. While I thoroughly enjoy all of the benefits and privileges of being one of God's children on this Earth, I often remind myself that "this is not all there is". I am not satisfied with what this world has to offer, and I guess that's why God tells us this from the Book of Revelation:

Then I saw "a new heaven and a new earth," for the first heaven and the first earth had passed away - Revelation 21:1 (NIV)

TODAY'S WISDOM NUGGET
"God loves a CHEERFUL giver" - 2 Cor. 9:7.
So, don't be a TEARFUL giver or a FEARFUL giver.
There's no need to cry or to be afraid when you give to God...
it's always a good investment!

JOY IN THE JOURNEY
April 6 | October 4

Life isn't always about destination... sometimes it's just as much about "the journey." When my kids were little we lived a short distance from a creek that ran through the woods. Every once in a while my kids would say to me, "Daddy, let's go on a 'venture'" (they couldn't say "adventure") and that always meant that they wanted to go down to the creek and explore. No, they weren't asking to just go to a PLACE. They had the choice of zoos, playgrounds, parks, and museums. They were asking to go to a HAPPENING. You see, every time we went to that creek there was something new to see or a new path to explore that we hadn't been on before. We never knew what we were in for until we got there and it happened... and that's what the kids liked most about going on a "venture."

We forget about stuff like that when we get older. We think life is all about arriving somewhere and fulfilling a goal, but sometimes it's just about enjoying the journey and the discoveries made along the way.

I remember one of our "ventures" very well. We were at the creek and the kids were looking at rocks while I was scouting out a new path to take. My daughter said, "Daddy, look at this rock!" You have to understand, we were standing on the bank of this creek and millions of rocks were washed up on the shore. I had already heard, "Look at this rock, Daddy" about a hundred times as both of my kids tried to capture my attention with their discoveries. But, since this is what we did on "ventures" I decided to look her way once again. She held in her hand a totally spherical rock, perfectly round... it was an old Indian marble that was crafted by some Native American hundreds of years ago. My little girl found an Indian artifact because she was taking the time to explore the world around her... while I was looking further down the trail.

To all who are looking "further down the trail" today... take time to enjoy what's on the path in front of you. That's where you find the "Joy in the Journey"!

1 Timothy 6:17 (NIV)
God... richly provides us with everything for our enjoyment.

YOUR SMILE FOR TODAY
"Ye are the salt of the earth" - Matthew 5:13.
Don't lose your saltiness or it will be "the bland leading the bland."

ECLIPSE OF THE SON
April 7 | October 5

Have you ever had a dream that was so "real" and life-like that it just stuck with you? Well, I had one of those dreams one morning right before I awoke from sleep. It was a dream about a solar eclipse. When I woke up I was able to immediately attach a meaning to the dream because of its clarity.

A solar eclipse is a baffling event! A small, insignificant, uninhabited orb, THE MOON, has the incredible ability to block the view, and the light of the enormous sun from us. Amazing! It's all about proximity. During a solar eclipse the moon is so close to Earth, and the sun so far away, that the sun is eclipsed by something that is just a fraction of it's size.

In the same way, The S-O-N is enormous and powerful beyond compare. But, a small, seemingly insignificant circumstance of life can appear to eclipse His power and brightness. So, how do we avoid a total eclipse of the Son? It's simple to say, but rather hard to do... we must not let anything stand between us and our Savior.

I think of Zaccheus... remember him? Zaccheus was a man of small stature who wanted to see Jesus, but couldn't see him or get to him because of the crowd of people surrounding Jesus. THE SON HAD BEEN ECLIPSED. But he didn't groan or complain! Instead, he found higher ground. He climbed up into a sycamore tree just so he could get a glimpse of the Savior. He refused to let the crowd obstruct his view of God's Son. His fortitude was recognized by Jesus and he was rewarded by the Master visiting his home.

Every day we are faced with things that try to obstruct our view of Jesus. We must be determined, just like Zaccheus, that nothing will stand in the way between us and the Master. We will not allow anything to Eclipse His brightness!

Hebrews 12:2 (Berean Study Bible)
Let us fix our eyes on Jesus

TODAY'S WORD OF ENCOURAGEMENT
You may not be highly educated, highly talented or highly qualified, but if you're highly FAVORED you're sure to succeed!
Luke 1:28 - "Rejoice, highly favored one, the Lord is with you..."

COME UP HERE!
April 8 | October 6

My son and I were walking on a concrete pathway along the South Rim of the Grand Canyon. After hiking along the path for about a mile or so we decided to head back. On our way back I noticed that we were now going "uphill." When we began our hike, I hadn't even noticed that the pathway was on a gradual "decline," but I sure did notice the gradual "incline" on the hike back as my heart was beating out of my chest and my lungs gasped for oxygen!

Sometimes in life we don't recognize the subtleties associated with a downward turn. Momentum gathers as we take the path of least resistance and eventually succumb to "lower living." The laws of science remind us that the pull of gravity downward is a force to be reckoned with, and can only be overcome with a resisting, opposing force. Did you know that it takes 302 muscles in your body, working together, for you to stand up? But, it doesn't take any muscular activity to fall... all you have to do to fall is simply release all your muscles. But who wants to fall? Yes, it takes some extra effort to stand but it sure beats falling down!

If you find yourself today in a "low place" I can empathize with you. I've been there myself. To overcome that low place, however, a resisting, opposing force must be exerted. Energy and effort must be released to overcome it.

Personally, when I'm feeling LOW, I often find inspiration in God's Word to pull me out of my slump. Philippians 3:14 says, "I press on toward the goal for the prize of the UPWARD call of God in Christ Jesus." When I'm tempted to go the path of least resistance I'm reminded of Hebrews 10:39, "But we are not of those who SHRINK BACK and are destroyed, but of those who believe and are saved." One of my favorite reminders that picks me up when I'm feeling low is found in Ephesians 2:6, "And God raised us UP with Christ and seated us with him in the heavenly realms in Christ Jesus."

There is no shame in admitting that you are in a low place, and the crazy thing is that you may not even be aware of how you got there. But you weren't created for "low living." so listen to the voice of God as He calls out to you like He did to John on the island of Patmos:

"Come UP here...." Rev. 4:1 (NIV)

JUST SEND YOUR WORD, LORD
April 9 | October 7

A chill went down my spine one night as I taught a Bible Study at the Men's Home. We were studying about the centurion who asked Jesus to come and heal his servant. While Jesus was still far off, the centurion sent word to Him to not come to his house, but to just "say the word and my servant will be healed." The Bible says that Jesus responded to this request in a most unusual way. It says, "He marveled at him." The word "marveled" here means "to be amazed, to have admiration for."

So, Jesus was amazed, and He admired this man. Why? Because of his faith. And how was his faith different from others? Well, up to this point in Jesus' ministry the only way people were getting healed by Him was by Jesus coming and putting His hands upon them, or by them touching Him or being in close connection to Him. You see, many had faith that Jesus could heal them, or their loved ones, if He were in the same proximity. Mary and Martha felt this way, for when after their brother Lazarus had died they said to Jesus, "If You had BEEN HERE he would not have died." Their faith in Jesus' ability was based on His proximity. He had to be close by, or at least touch the sick individual for the healing to take place. But, here is a man, the centurion, who had faith that said, "YOU DON'T EVEN HAVE TO BE HERE TO HEAL... JUST SEND YOUR WORD!" No one had ever asked Jesus to heal in this way before. It was a powerful demonstration of faith that truly AMAZED JESUS.

Now, here's where the chill went down my spine. It hit me, as I was teaching this, that you and I are much like the centurion. When we pray for the sick to be healed or for any type of need, we, in essence, are saying, "Lord, you're not here walking on the earth now... but You don't have to be here 'in the flesh' to perform a miracle... we believe that You can send Your Word to do the job!" That is the kind of faith that AMAZED Jesus 2,000 years ago... and I believe it still does!

Psalms 107:20
He sent his word, and healed them

TODAY'S WORD OF ENCOURAGEMENT
Diamonds can be produced synthetically in a high-pressure, high-temperature process which simulates the conditions in the Earth's mantle. Are you in a high-pressure situation? You may be a "diamond" in the making!

INSPIRATION
April 10 | October 8

Several years ago I started a little graphic design business and I wanted to have some reference to the thought that my design work is not just my own ideas, but rather a collaboration between me and the God who inspires me with His creativity. Thus, I decided to name the business INSPIRED Design and Graphics.

In most dictionaries, the first definition for the word "inspired" that you'll find will say something to this effect: "to affect, guide or arouse by divine influence." That was the definition I had in mind.... that God influences me in my work. But it was not until recently, through some random sequence of events, that I came to realize that the word INSPIRED means so much more than that.

I heard someone say the word "RESPIRATION" and it triggered the word "INSPIRATION" in my mind. Both words have the same root word. Could it be that inspiration and respiration are closely related? So I looked up the word INSPIRE in the dictionary. Sure enough, one of the definitions for INSPIRE is "to breathe on, to breathe life into."

When God created Adam the Bible says that He "breathed into his nostrils the breath of life and man became a living being." It wasn't until God INSPIRED man (breathed life into him) that he actually became a living being! Unfortunately, when Adam and Eve sinned they "got the BREATH knocked out of them" so to speak. But when Jesus came and died on the cross and rose from the dead He did something unusual to His disciples... He BREATHED on them (John 20:22). The BREATH (inspiration) that was lost because of man's sin was restored once again. So I am happy to announce to you today that I am INSPIRED... I've had life breathed into me. What about you?

2 Timothy 3:16
All Scripture is INSPIRED [breathed into] by God and profitable for teaching, for reproof, for correction, for training in righteousness

TODAY'S FOOD FOR THOUGHT
When you are thankful you'll keep your tank full.
When you're complaining your tank is draining.
"Be thankful unto him, and bless his name." Psalm 100:4

PUSH THROUGH AND DO IT ANYWAY
April 11 | October 9

Several years ago part of my morning routine was to take a two-mile jog each morning. I did it as a form of exercise and for health reasons. I was talking to a friend about my exercise routine and explained to him that some mornings I jogged while other mornings I just walked. He asked why I walked instead of jogged and I said, "Because some mornings I just don't feel like jogging." He just smiled, let out a little chuckle and said, "Well Greg, when you don't FEEL like it, that's when you just push through and do it anyway."

Those simple words reverberated over and over again in my mind just about every morning for the next several months. When I woke up in the morning and contemplated whether I would jog or walk I would hear my friend's words, "When you don't feel like it just push through and do it anyway". So, even when I didn't feel like jogging, I pushed through and did it anyway, and I felt so much better for having done so.

Inspiring words don't always have to be profound.... sometimes they can be as simple as "When you don't feel like it, just do it anyway." As I heard those words reverberating in my mind each morning they motivated me to do something I didn't really want to do. Wow! Inspiring words have so much power!

With that thought in mind today, I say to you: "You may not FEEL like doing the right thing today, but just push through and do it anyway. You may not FEEL like being nice to others who mistreat you, but just push through and do it anyway. You may not FEEL like being positive when everybody else is being negative, but just push through and do it anyway." When you do the right thing even when you don't really FEEL like it there is something special that happens to you.... you become AN OVERCOMER!

1 John 5:4 (NAS)
For whatever is born of God OVERCOMES the world; and this is the victory that has overcome the world - our faith.

TODAY'S ENCOURAGING WORD
I believe I CAN DO ANYTHING I set my mind to do.
I also believe I CAN DO NOTHING... unless God empowers me.
I can do all things through Christ who gives me strength. - Phil 4:13

TWO PLUS TWO IS....
April 12 | October 10

We've heard it o'er and o'er
That "Two plus two is four"
And there's no other answer we can derive.
In attempts to make things "new"
What if they told you "Two plus two
Is no longer four... it is now five."

Would you change what you believe
Even though you can't conceive
How the answer could be anything but FOUR?
What if they labeled you a "hater"
And criticized, "Your way's not greater!"
Would you cave-in to the pressure of their roar?

Would it be worth a fight
To ensure the answer's right?
Would you say "four's the answer," no matter the cost?
For soon their "new-found knowledge"
Will be taught in schools and college
And to the whole next generation truth is lost.

Well, I hate to rock the boat
And I'd rather stay afloat
But there are some things with which I can't agree.
I have a firm persuasion
That the answer to the equation
Forever will be FOUR... not FIVE or THREE.

Now, just like "two plus two"
The Bible speaks to me and you
With truths throughout the ages that survive.
So if even government
Says "Truth has changed" I won't relent
I remember "two plus two is four... not five."

TODAY'S FOOD FOR THOUGHT
Imitation may be the highest form of Flattery, but it's the lowest
form of Creativity! Don't imitate...ORIGINATE!

AN ENCOURAGING WORD
April 13 | October 11

One Sunday morning in church an African-American lady sat down on the row in front of me with her two teenage daughters and preteen son. I had never met this family in the church before and did not know if they were regular attenders or not. During the "get acquainted" portion of the service the two girls turned to me and offered a handshake, a smile and a friendly "Good Morning." I then offered a handshake and greeting to the mother and son.

During the Worship Service one of the daughters was crying, visibly moved, either by the music and worship or by something she was dealing with in her heart. The mother and other daughter put their hands on her back, giving her loving strokes as they continued to worship. I watched as the boy would look over with concern on his face toward his sister. I was impressed by the amount of care and compassion this little family displayed.

When the service was over I reached forward and touched the mother's shoulder. "Is this your family?" I asked, trying to develop a conversation. She smiled big and replied, "Yes, these are my 2 daughters and my son." I said, "You sure do have a sweet family." Tears welled up in her eyes as she said, "Thank you." I went on, "You're doing a great job raising these kids. I can tell by the way they care about each other." I don't know all that transferred from my lips to her ears and into her heart at that moment, but tears began to flow down her cheeks as she repeatedly replied, "Thank you, Thank you. You don't know how much a single mother needs to hear that." I didn't know that she was a single mother... but God did. I gave her a big hug and we parted ways, but I left with this thought in my mind and heart: Never underestimate the power of an encouraging word spoken at just the right moment.

Proverbs 16:24
Pleasant words are as an honeycomb, sweet to the soul, and health to the bones.

TODAY'S WISDOM NUGGET
When your mouth is speaking, your heart is leaking. *"Out of the abundance of the heart the mouth speaks." Matthew 12:34.*

GROW!
April 14 | October 12

What are the only recorded ages of Jesus found in the Bible? 12 and 30. At the age of 12 we find Jesus in the temple talking with the elders and Pharisees and astounding them with his wisdom (Luke 2:42). In Luke 3:23 the Bible tells us that Jesus was about 30 years old when he started his ministry. So what about the 18 years of his life from age 12 to 30? Were they important? What did he do? The only thing we know for sure about those years is what is recorded in Luke 2:52, "And Jesus grew in wisdom and stature and in favor with God and man."

There are many young people these days who are struggling with their direction in life. They thought that by the age of 18, 19, or 20 they should have some firm sense of direction, some feeling of purpose and destiny. Instead, they feel like nothing is happening for them, and that their lives are aimless and direction-less. But if the Son of God didn't make any headlines between the ages of 12 and 30 there isn't any reason to put undue pressure on yourself. The important thing to remember is that Jesus "grew in wisdom and stature and in favor with God and man." And that's the best thing that a young person can do while they are waiting on their destiny to unfold.

1. GROW in WISDOM (learn from those who have already learned in life)...
2. GROW in STATURE (take care of your body and keep it healthy and strong)...
3. GROW in FAVOR WITH GOD AND MAN (live the kind of life that God would put His blessing upon, and that men would give their seal of approval on.)

It is these small things that you do now (just like Jesus did in his 20s) that will pave the way for your future no matter what your destiny might be. So, take a lesson from Jesus when He was in his 20s... GROW!

Job 8:7 "Though thy beginning was small, yet thy latter end should greatly increase."

TODAY'S WISDOM NUGGET
The cure for a heavy heart is a GOOD WORD. *"Anxiety in a man's heart weighs it down, But a good word makes it glad." Proverbs 12:25*

"MEAT TO EAT THAT YOU KNOW NOT OF"
April 15 | October 13

Several years ago I put together a reunion of the former members of the Church where I was born again (Trinity Chapel in Decatur, Alabama). It was an awesome time of getting reacquainted and reminiscing. After our fellowship supper Pastor Rabon Stewart got up and shared his heart about the beginnings of the church. One thing that stuck in my mind was something he said near the end. He mentioned the fellowship meals that we regularly had together as a church family, and how he many times would be the very last one to get served because he was busy fellowshipping with people. Someone came up to him on one occasion and said, "Pastor Rabon if you don't hurry up and get in line to get something to eat all the food will be gone!" Repeating the words of Jesus, Rabon simply replied, "I have meat to eat that you know not of!"

I have been a Christian now for four decades, and I have seen a lot of good, and some of the "not so good," that goes on in the church. I've seen leaders who've led with a heavy hand. I've seen those who expected special treatment and favoritism, to get pushed to the front of the line to get V.I.P. seating. But, I'm so thankful that my first understanding of Church leadership came from this humble servant of God, Rabon Stewart... not requiring special honor, not commanding attention or demanding first place in line... just loving and serving.

Thank you Pastor Rabon for being such a good example of Christian leadership to so many people. Thank you for showing us the true meaning of Jesus' words, "The first shall be last and the last shall be first." Throughout my Christian life I have never considered being "in the back of the line" as a bad thing. So many times over the years at church fellowship dinners I have naturally gravitated to the back of the line as I fellowshipped with those who waited. Although I was a "leader" in the church it was not beneath me to wait patiently as I emulated the servant's heart of my mentor... Pastor Rabon Stewart.

Yes, I too have "*meat to eat that you know not of.*" *(John 4:32)*

TODAY'S WISDOM NUGGET
Give God what's His and He will give you what's yours.
"*Seek ye first the kingdom of God and His righteousness, and all these things will be added unto you.*" Matthew 6:33

LYING DORMANT
April 16 | October 14

While on my morning prayer walk I was praying for a family member and these words came out of my mouth without any forethought: "Reveal to them the things that still lie dormant within them that have not yet been manifested." That wording took me by surprise... I don't ever recall praying for anyone like that before so I believe these words were inspired from Heaven.

Imagine that! There are things within you and me (talents, giftings, insights, businesses, ideas, etc.) that are lying dormant... not yet revealed because the proper time has not yet come, OR because we have not been willing to step out of our comfort zone and rise to the new level that God is calling us to.

It is wrong to hold to the belief about yourself that you are a "completed work" and that there is nothing more to be revealed in you. With this thought in mind, I have come to the conclusion that there are 2 groups of people in life...

1.) Those who think that they are currently complete, a finished work, and thus will not go any further in developing as a person.
2.) Those who see themselves as being in a continual growth process where something new and fresh could manifest at any given moment.

God is a great big God. He is creative and imaginative. If He's working on you and me there's no way that His work in us is finished. So, I'm getting prepared for some new things to be revealed in my life... things that have been lying dormant, but are about to be manifested! How about you?

Philippians 1:6 (NAS)
For I am confident of this very thing, that He who began a good work in you will perfect it until the day of Christ Jesus.

TODAY'S FOOD FOR THOUGHT
"Let this CUP pass from me:
nevertheless not as I will, but as thou wilt." Matt. 26:39.
As your cup of blessing overflows, remember... the only reason your cup is full is because Jesus switched cups with you!

DAMAGED... BUT STILL USEFUL
April 17 | October 15

I was reaching for the bar of soap one morning and noticed that there was a big gash on one of its corners. From the looks of things it was easy to figure out that someone dropped the soap and that it had taken a pretty good fall to sustain so much damage. But I didn't throw the bar away... I still used it in spite of the gash. The soap's purpose had not been negated just because it had been damaged.

There are people all around, much like that bar of soap, who've taken a fall in life and were left damaged as a result. But, a fall doesn't nullify a person's purpose or negate the gifting that is within them. Your purpose and your calling didn't change because you took a spill. Yes, you may be bruised and you may bear the marks of that fall, but your purpose remains in tact. Receive encouragement from this verse of scripture found in the Message Bible in Romans 11:29: *"God's gifts and God's call are under full warranty - never canceled, never rescinded."*

WHY DO INNOCENT PEOPLE SUFFER?

I've heard people ask, "If God is a loving God why do innocent people suffer?" I'll answer that question with my own question: "Do people in Heaven suffer?" The answer is NO! Heaven is the place where God's complete and perfect will is performed, not Earth. It is for this reason Jesus encouraged us to pray to the Father, "Your kingdom come, Your will be done ON EARTH AS IT IS IN HEAVEN." There is pain and suffering on Earth because God's Will is not consistently performed on Earth, and at least part of the reason for that is because people are not praying for God's Will to be done on Earth as it is in Heaven. We must be willing to accept our responsibility and cooperate with God to see His influence on Earth. So, I leave us with this question: "If we are loving people why do we let innocent people suffer as we continue to avoid prayer?"

Matthew 6:10 (NIV)
Your kingdom come, your will be done, on earth as it is in heaven.

TODAY'S WISDOM NUGGET
Heb.11:24 "BY FAITH Moses, when he was come to years, REFUSED TO BE CALLED the son of Pharaoh's daughter" When you walk by faith there are some things you must REFUSE TO BE CALLED.

I'VE ALREADY HEARD THAT!
April 18 | October 16

One day I was teaching a Sunday School class of elementary kids and one little boy complained, "I've already heard this story!" So, did I stop there and come up with another lesson? NO! Some things you need to hear more than once to get it down in your heart and not just in your mind... and that's what I told the little boy.

I'd like to change a familiar scripture verse to make a point. Here goes: Romans 10:17, "So then faith cometh by hearing and hearing by the word of God." Did you catch the change in this verse? You didn't?! All I did was remove a comma after the first "hearing"... that was the only change. So now you're saying "Faith comes by hearing and hearing" not just "Faith comes by hearing." Let me put it this way: Knowledge comes by hearing, but faith comes by hearing and hearing. We've got enough "knowledgeable people" already. What we need is more "faith people." Faith people don't get bored with hearing the same thing more than once.

When I was a kid, my math teacher didn't say 2+2=4 just one time. She said it over and over again until it sank down deep into me. After she said 2+2=4 for the third time I could have easily said, "Teacher, I've already heard this. Let's move on to Algebra now!" But, I needed to hear it quite a few more times to the point where it was no longer "knowledge" that I had obtained but something that flowed out of me without even having to think about it.

So, ask yourself this question today: "Do I have knowledge of God's Word or do I have faith in God's Word?" There IS a difference. Let's face it. There are some things we need to hear more than once to build our faith... we need to hear it over and over again... and that "thing" we need to hear is the Word of God.

Romans 10:8 (NIV)
But what does it say? "The word is near you; it is in your mouth and in your heart," that is, the message concerning faith that we proclaim

TODAY'S WISDOM NUGGET
"Let the weak say, I am strong." Joel 3:10
When you're feeling weak, but you say "I am strong" you're not denying your current "reality"... you're creating a new one!

IT'S A HURDLE... NOT A WALL!
April 19 | October 17

Some people mistake a hurdle for a wall. When you meet with a hurdle in life you simply jump over it. You don't have to be intimidated by it and you don't have to stop your race because it's there. You might find this interesting. The 400 meter hurdles event incorporates 10 hurdles that are evenly spaced along the track. Runners must run the full 400 meters PLUS clear 10 hurdles in the process. Now, get this... the world record for the 400 meter "run" is 43.18 seconds. The world record for the 400 meter "hurdles" is 46.78 seconds... only 3 seconds more! Same distance, PLUS jumping over 10 hurdles along the way! Don't let it stop you in your race... it's just a hurdle... GET OVER IT!

Hebrews 12:1 "let us lay aside every weight, and the sin which doth so easily beset us, and let us run with patience the race that is set before us,"

NOTHING COULD MAKE ME HAPPIER

When I was in my 20s and Christmas was getting close I would go to my Dad and ask, "What do you want for Christmas this year, Dad?" His reply was always the same, year after year, "I just want all my kids to be happy." There was 5 of us kids, and he had seen all of us go through our share of heartache and troubles. Being a father of 2 myself, I now know what my Dad was saying. Nothing makes me happier than to see my kids happy. And, I suppose this holds true for all fathers who love their kids deeply. Fathers didn't get this "instinct" all on their own, though. The very first father (GOD) is the One who put this desire within us. In 3 John 1:4, God tells us through the apostle John, "I have NO GREATER JOY than to hear that my children are walking in the truth." A good father's greatest joy is to know that his kids are happy. And, how do they get happy? The above verse gives the answer: "By walking in the truth". So, Dads, if your kids come to you in the upcoming days and ask, "What do you want for Christmas this year?" tell them, "I just want all my kids to walk in the truth... nothing could make me happier!"

YOUR SMILE FOR TODAY
I remember a time when going to God in prayer was my "last resort."
Now it's my first resort, my second resort, and every other resort.
I guess you could say I spend most of my time "at the resort!"

FIND THE HONEYSUCKLE VINE
April 20 | October 18

On one of my morning walks I came upon a honeysuckle vine in full bloom and stopped to enjoy the beauty and aroma that it offered. Moments later I came upon a poison ivy vine… and avoided it completely.

That's what we've got to do in life. Enjoy the beauty… take it in and inhale the aroma of the good and the pleasant. At the same time, we must be aware that the unpleasant does exist, but we don't have to dwell on it, stand over it, examine it and involve ourselves in it to the point where we forget about the beauty. That's like putting poison ivy up to your nose and sniffing it when a honeysuckle vine is just a few feet away.

I've seen many people whose take on life is so negative and skeptical because they immerse themselves in the ugly and the unpleasant things that are going on in our world. They're standing in a patch of poison ivy, wondering why they're so irritated (and itchy). Look for the honeysuckle vine… it's there. Yes, I know terrible things are going on in the world. My head is not stuck in the sand…but it is stuck in the honeysuckle vine.

"LORD, I LOVE YOU"

Lord, I know that I've failed you, misinterpreted you and even misrepresented you… but I LOVE YOU. There have been times I've ignored you, avoided you and probably even angered you… but I LOVE YOU. Like Judas, I've betrayed you and like Peter, I've denied You.. but I LOVE YOU. I'm the deficient one in this relationship. I'm the one with the faults, shortcomings and character flaws… but I LOVE YOU. I read in Your Word that LOVE covers a multitude of sins, and I'm pretty sure it's YOUR LOVE that verse is referring to. But, today, when You look at me, I pray that you won't see all of my faults, failures and sins… I pray that my LOVE FOR YOU will cover all of them. I think about how Peter failed you when he denied You three times, and how you restored him when You asked him three times, "DO YOU LOVE ME?" Ask me the same question, Lord. You know the answer…LORD, I LOVE YOU.

TODAY'S FOOD FOR THOUGHT
You know you're a "lover of truth" when you would rather hear a truth that makes you feel uncomfortable than a lie that makes you feel good.

MAN UP!
April 21 | October 19

One of my favorite Bible verses for men is found in the book of Job. In Job 3:8 God said to Job, "Now gird up your loins like a man…." Put in today's vernacular, God was saying "MAN UP!" I asked a group of men at a Bible Study, "If God came to you and said 'Man Up' what would you assume about yourself at that moment?" One man answered, "I would assume that I had not been acting like a man." Exactly! So, the question arises, "What does a real man look like and act like?" Over the past decades I have heard sayings such as REAL MEN don't eat quiche, REAL MEN don't cry, REAL MEN don't drive mini-vans, etc. etc. I'm not really interested in this world's definition of what a REAL MAN is, though. I just want to know what God's definition of a REAL MAN is. Looking at God's design of the very first man, Adam, here are a few things I believe God considers a REAL MAN to be:

1. Somebody who reflects God's image and glory on the Earth (after all, God did say "Let us make man in our own IMAGE" Genesis 1:26).
2. Somebody who has power and authority over his domain ("…and let them rule over the fish of the sea and the birds of the air, over the livestock, over all the earth…" Genesis 1:26)
3. Somebody who is fruitful and duplicates himself in the Earth (and God said "Be fruitful and multiply…" Genesis 1:28)
4. Somebody who knows how to work, and how to protect what's been given to him ("Then the Lord God took the man and put him in the garden of Eden to tend and keep it." Genesis 2:15)

So, armed with this information, here's what a REAL MAN looks like: A person who looks like and acts like God no matter what He's facing in life… A person who has authority and takes responsibility… A person who is interested in producing and raising up a generation who will follow in his footsteps… and a person who will work hard and protect/defend what God gives him. When God sees any man behaving in a fashion that is beneath these attributes of a REAL MAN He has the right to say "MAN UP!"

YOUR SMILE FOR TODAY
One day, when you've breathed your last breath, they'll put your body in a box and bury you. Up until that moment… think outside the box.

LOWERED TO OUR LEVEL
April 22 | October 20

I am 6ft 3in tall. When I reach my hand upwards as high as it can go the tips of my fingers reach the 8ft mark. Now, the average height of the kids in my Wednesday night class at church is about 4ft 3in. Sometimes when the kids have done well at something in the class I'll say, "That was good… give me a high five!" and then I'll stretch my hand upwards to that 8ft mark. It's fun seeing the creativity they will use in their attempt to give me a "high" five. Some will get a running start and jump. Others will climb on to a chair. Still others will grab my arm and try to pull my hand down to a level that they can reach. Some of the taller kids can actually jump up and touch my wrist and then exclaim, "I did it!" but ultimately my outstretched hand is out of everyone's reach. No one is successful. So, I eventually lower my hand down to a place where everyone can hit it because I want them all to have success. I guess you could say that I "come down to their level."

In Isaiah 55:8-9 God says, "For as the heavens are higher than the earth, So are My ways higher than your ways and My thoughts than your thoughts." Throughout history, man's attempts to get on "God's level" have been futile, much like my elementary kids who try to give me a high five when my hand is fully outstretched upwards. Romans 3:23 reminds us that "all have sinned and FALL SHORT of the glory of God." Truly, some have reached higher than others, but all attempts have ultimately ended in failure. So, what did God do? He came down to our level. He took on flesh and bone and became one of us so we could have success in our attempt to reach out to Him. Jesus was "God in the flesh." Though He was the HIGH and LOFTY ONE He humbled himself and walked among us so we could touch Him. So, remember this: The success we achieve in reaching out to God is not because of our human effort but because He lowered himself to our level, in an attempt to raise us up to His!

Philippians 2:8 (NIV)
And being found in appearance as a man, he humbled himself

TODAY'S WISDOM NUGGET
Your happiness in your relationships (this side of Heaven) is directly proportional to your ability to tolerate imperfections.
"Above all, love each other deeply, because love covers over a multitude of sins." 1 Peter 4:8

FAITH... AND MICROWAVE OVENS
April 23 | October 21

A young man told me, "I shouldn't have been baptized when I was 6 years old. I was too young and didn't understand what I was doing." He continued to talk about how children aren't knowledgeable enough to make a decision of that magnitude until they get old enough to understand it better. I remained quiet as he talked.

When he was finished I asked a question, "Do you understand how a microwave oven works? He replied, "No." I asked, "Do you understand how you can take something out of a freezer, stick it in the microwave oven, turn it on and in just a minute or so can pull out a piping hot piece of food without the use of a fire or heating elements?" Again, he replied, "No." So, I asked a third question, "Do you have to understand how a microwave works in order to use it... to take advantage of what it offers?" And again he replied, "No."

I still had more questions to ask so I continued, "Do you understand how God raised Jesus from the dead?" He replied, "No." I told him, "Yet, the Bible tells us in Romans 10:9-10 that a person has to believe that God raised Christ from the dead in order to be saved." (Notice that it said BELIEVE, not UNDERSTAND). I don't understand how HE did it either, but I do believe it, and that's what God requires.

There is a simple reason why God tells us in Proverbs 3:5-6 "Lean not unto your own understanding." It's because there are too many things we don't understand. But, I can "believe" even when I can't "understand." So, I don't walk by my understanding... I walk by faith (2 Cor. 5:7). Faith puts everyone on a level playing field. A child can believe just as easily as an adult. A poor person can believe just as easily as a rich person. An ignorant person can believe just as easily as an educated person. "Faith" excludes no one. "Understanding" excludes large quantities of people. So, don't lean on your own understanding. It's insufficient. Instead, walk by faith! You now have permission to use your microwave oven.

Proverbs 3:5 - "lean not unto thine own understanding."

TODAY'S ENCOURAGING WORD
God notices the tears you cry. He keeps record of them. David wrote: *"Put my tears in Thy bottle; Are they not in Thy Book?" Psalm 56:8*

FATHER, FORGIVE THEM
April 24 | October 22

I saw something sort of strange happen one night right before my eyes. I saw a tow truck cause a wreck. He rear-ended the car in front of him and pushed it into another car. No one was hurt, fortunately. It's sort of ironic when you think about it. Here's a guy that we call on for help when we're in a wreck, and he actually caused a wreck himself.

If you live long enough you'll see strange things like this happen throughout your life. People who are supposed to help others sometimes actually hurt them instead. Most of the time they don't even mean to. It just happens. I've seen doctors (people that are called to bring healing) wound people. I've seen teachers (people that are called to bring understanding) confuse people. I've even seen pastors (people that are called to bring encouragement) discourage people. Perhaps you've been hurt by someone that was supposed to help... you're not alone.

I think about Jesus. He came to a people who should have welcomed him as their Messiah... instead they rejected Him. He came to priests who should have honored and respected him... they spit on him and insulted him. Pilate, a man who could have ordered Jesus' release, pronounced his death sentence. And, the soldiers who were supposed to be protectors of the peace crucified the Prince of Peace. Nobody did the right thing by Jesus, yet, as He hung there upon the cross he prayed that the Father would forgive those who were mistreating Him.

I don't know your story. I don't know who did you wrong. I don't know if it was on purpose or just an accident. But, I do know this: you have in no way been mistreated in the same manner as Jesus... the son of God, treated like a common criminal. Yet, he offered forgiveness, even in the middle of His mistreatment. So, I leave you with this thought for today: There is no greater revelation that a person can have about forgiving others than this...

"Father, forgive them for they know not what they do." - Luke 23:34

TODAY'S FOOD FOR THOUGHT
A voice without love is NOTHING - 1 Cor. 13:1.
A gift without love is NOTHING - 1 Cor.13:2.
A sacrifice without love is NOTHING - 1 Cor. 13:3.

LET YOUR CONTENTS SHOW!
April 25 | October 23

I held two seemingly identical coffee mugs up in the air at the Men's Home Bible Study. I asked the men if they could see any difference between the two mugs. They all agreed that the two mugs were practically identical in appearance. So, I said, "So, if I told you I was going to give you one of these mugs to keep would you have a preference as to which one it was?" They all agreed that it would make no difference to them which one I gave them. "That's a shame" I said, "because if you had chosen this one (I tipped one of the mugs over and poured out a wad of cash on the floor) look what you would have received!" They all laughed and then admitted that the contents of the mugs was just as important as the outward appearance. I then tipped the other mug over to reveal that it was completely empty.

Today, many will see you and make judgments and estimations about you solely based on your outward appearance and actions. You will not be able to avoid this. But, before you part ways hopefully they will find out that there is more to you "than meets the eye." 2 Corinthians 4:7 says, "But we have this treasure in earthen vessels (clay pots), so that the surpassing greatness of the power will be of God and not from ourselves." You may look like all the other "clay pots" around, but if you'll let the treasure within you shine many will realize that there is something different about you... because your contents are showing.

My Prayer for Today:
"Lord, I may just be a clay pot, but because You are in me I'm filled with greatness and goodness. May my "contents" show today in every aspect of my life. May others see YOU in ME. "

1 John 4:4
Greater is He that is IN YOU than he that is in the world.

TODAY'S FOOD FOR THOUGHT

Could it be that the aching dissatisfaction that you sometimes feel in life is just a subtle reminder that this is not your permanent dwelling place? There's no place like home... and this is NOT it.
"But now they desire a better country, that is, an heavenly: wherefore God is not ashamed to be called their God: for he hath prepared for them a city." Hebrews 11:16

WHERE IS THIS ROAD TAKING YOU?
April 26 | October 24

I asked a troubled and rebellious young man, "Do you believe in prophets?" He replied, "Yes." I told him, "Well, I'm not one, but I can tell you your future right now because I can see the road you're traveling on, and it's the road that leads to jail and prison." I wasn't trying to scare the boy, nor was I trying to intimidate him. I was just being completely honest with him based on the things I could see going on in his life at the moment. He told me he would be okay and wouldn't do anything stupid enough to wind up in prison.

We parted ways and I continued to pray for him. I got a voice message from him just two days later, saying, "I got busted last night and I'm in a detention center." Talk about prophesy fulfilled! But, as I mentioned, I'm not a prophet... however, I can tell what the future holds for a person just by looking at the road they're traveling on. It's not rocket science.

Going straight through the middle of my hometown there's a highway called Highway 31. If I saw you driving south on Highway 31 I could make some fairly accurate assumptions about where you were headed. You might be headed to Falkville, or a little further south to Cullman or perhaps even a little further south to Birmingham. That's where that highway takes the motorists on it. So, here's how I can "prophesy" your future:

1.) I see the road you're traveling on, and
2.) I see the direction in which you're heading.
The rest is elementary!

With this in mind ask yourself this question: "What road am I on right now, and where is it headed? What would be the final destination if I continued on this road without making a u-turn?" No, you don't have to be a prophet to be able to tell your future. Just take a look at the road that you've been traveling on... and see where it is headed.

Proverbs 14:12 (International Standard Version)
There is a pathway that seems right to a man, but in the end it's a road to death.

TODAY'S FOOD FOR THOUGHT
"Absence makes the heart grow fonder." - Man
"My Presence makes the heart grow fonder." - God

ASCEND!
April 27 | October 25

I saw a scene unfold on my morning walk that I've only seen on just a couple of other occasions... A crow and a hawk in aerial battle. Crows are hawk's worst enemies. Evidently the soaring hawk got just a little too close to the crow's territory so the crow chased the hawk from behind and was "dive-bombing" him. The chase went on for several minutes but I knew what was going to happen next. I've seen it played out on the other occasions when I've witnessed this same battle. Slowly and methodically the hawk caught currents that took him to higher altitudes. It took a little bit of time to make the adjustments so the crow "got his licks in" during the process. But, as the hawk circled higher and higher he finally got out of the crow's comfort zone so the crow retreated back down to a lower altitude. Lesson learned? When dealing with an irritating and annoying enemy go to higher altitudes! If you stay on a level where your enemy is comfortable you will be in for a longer battle. Are you dealing with an enemy who is bringing you down? ASCEND!

Ephesians 2:6 (NIV)
And God raised us up with Christ and seated us with him in the heavenly realms in Christ Jesus.

HOLD YOUR PEACE!

Have you ever heard the phrase, "Let him speak now or forever HOLD HIS PEACE"? It is often used in wedding ceremonies. Isn't that an interesting phrase "HOLD YOUR PEACE?" Did you know you have a PEACE that you carry with you? When you refrain from speaking you are "holding your peace." So, remember, sometimes finding peace can be just as simple as keeping your mouth shut.

Proverbs 29:11
A fool uttereth all his mind: but a wise man keepeth it in till afterwards.

TODAY'S FOOD FOR THOUGHT
Genesis 2:9 "And out of the ground made the LORD God to GROW every tree that is pleasant to the sight."
God didn't create trees "full-grown"... He made them to GROW. And, humans don't come out of the womb full-grown! So, show the people in your life a little mercy... they'll begin to "GROW" on you!

THE OLD AND THE NEW
April 28 | October 26

I led worship at a small church one Sunday and had a good time mingling some newer worship choruses with some old familiar hymns. You might not think you could mix "Trading My Sorrows" with "Victory in Jesus" but it definitely can be done. When the service was over an older saint, whom I respect greatly, thanked me for blending the old with the new. As soon as those words left her mouth I immediately thought of the following verse from the Bible:

Matthew 13:52
Therefore every scribe who has become a disciple of the kingdom of heaven is like a head of a household, who brings out of his treasure things new and old.

Now, even though it is true that you can't put new wine into old wineskins you still need to have some "old" wine sometimes. After all, people don't walk into a restaurant and say, "Bring me your finest bottle of wine" and expect a bottle made last month.

People these days have forgotten the importance of "the old" as they try to find "something new." But, here's what I believe: we need new things to explore and discover while we stand on the foundation of old things that are proven and established over the years. The scribe, referred to in the above verse, is mentioned as having a treasure that he brings both new and old things from... a TREASURE! What kind of fool would throw out a 100 year old gold coin because "it's old!" Nonsense! We must learn to appreciate both the new and the old things that God has placed in our lives.

While on this subject, let me also mention this. Every person needs to have two influences in their lives: 1.) People younger than themselves that have a fresh perspective in life, and 2.) People older than themselves that have a track record of past experiences from which to draw counsel. To ignore either of these groups of people is to limit your future potential. So, with this in mind, why not go volunteer to help out in your church nursery... and when you're done there, go visit a nursing home.

TODAY'S FOOD FOR THOUGHT
Joy does not come from what is happening locally, nationally or globally... it comes from what is happening internally. (John 15:11)

THOU ANOINTEST MY HEAD WITH OIL
April 29 | October 27

I was teaching my kids at church from Psalm 23. I shared with them how a good shepherd will take care of his sheep by anointing their heads with oil (something like linseed oil). This oil is applied to ward off pesky insects that bother the sheep, and often lay eggs in their nasal passages and eyes. Sheep need to have their heads anointed to keep them safe from these annoyances. A good shepherd takes care of this job.

After sharing this information with the kids I told them that since I was like their shepherd, and they were my little lambs, I was going to anoint each one of their heads with oil. I explained, "I'm just going to put my finger in anointing oil and dab it on your forehead. Then I'll pray a prayer of blessing over each one of you, that your cup will run over with blessings and that your future will be blessed and prosperous." The fun began!

Everyone wanted to be a part. Kids are so receptive! One boy wanted me to anoint his head making the shape of a cross with the oil (a reasonable request) and one little boy said, "Do a car on my head" (Priceless moments in children's ministry… and yes, I obliged him). One by one they all came before me and allowed me to anoint their heads with oil as I prayed for a prosperous future, filled with favor and blessings for each one of them. It was such a reverent moment… one that I will never forget… especially because of what happened after I anointed the last child.

With my job as the "shepherd" completed, one of the little boys said, "Now, it's our turn to anoint you Mr. Greg" and all the kids agreed, "Yes, we want to anoint you with oil, too!" They sat me down in a chair and one little boy said a few sentences of appreciation about me (a blessing, if you will) as each child put a dab of oil on my head. What a moment in time. The sheep blessed the shepherd. And isn't that just the way it's supposed to be?

The Good Shepherd takes good care of us (His sheep) and in appreciation for His blessings we should in turn bless the Good Shepherd. I taught my little lambs a lesson that Wednesday night… then they taught me.

TODAY'S FOOD FOR THOUGHT
You may feel small and insignificant, but remember this: even the seemingly insignificant pawn, when used strategically, can put the King in checkmate! *Joel 3:10 - "Let the weak say, I am strong."*

1 OUT OF 10

April 30 | October 28

I conducted a chapel service at an elementary school a couple of years ago where I asked for 10 volunteers from the audience. When I had all 10 kids standing in front of me I said, "How many of you like Snickers candy bars?" They all eagerly raised their hands. Then I said, "I'm about to conduct an experiment. Hold out your hand and I'm going to give you a Snickers candy bar." Smiles abounded. I then placed a fun-size Snickers candy bar into each child's outstretched hand. When all 10 kids had a candy bar in their hands I turned around and said, "The experiment is over, you may be seated." There were questioning looks directed at me as the children took the Snickers bars with them to their seats.

What those children didn't know was that the goal of the experiment was to see how many would say "Thank you" upon receiving the candy bar. Interestingly enough only one child said "Thank you" when I put the candy bar in his hand. I then told the audience what the goal of the experiment was, and what the results were. A couple of the teachers in the audience looked upset that their kids didn't say "Thank you" after receiving the candy bar. But I told them, "Please don't get upset. You see, the results of my experiment are the same results that Jesus got when he healed the 10 lepers in Luke chapter 17. Only one returned to give Him thanks." I then proceeded to tell the story of the 10 lepers to the children and admonished them to always give God thanks for His good gifts.

You may very well be a part of a similar experiment today. God will be sending good things your way… dropping little blessings of His love and favor directly into your hands, just waiting to hear simple words of appreciation come from your mouth. What will your response be?

1 Thessalonians 5:18 (NAS)
In everything give thanks; for this is God's will for you in Christ Jesus.

TODAY'S FOOD FOR THOUGHT

If we asked "victorious" Bible characters what their greatest moment was the results might surprise us. Shadrach, Meshach and Abednego would say it was "a fiery furnace." Daniel would probably say "a lion's den" and Paul's reply might be "a Philippian jail cell."
The great moment in their lives came out of a time of great difficulty. Going through a tough time? A "great moment" could be ahead!

FINISHED
May 1 | October 29

Here's just a slightly different look at things. In Genesis 1, after every day of God's creative work, each day concluded with this thought: "And God saw that IT WAS GOOD." The sixth day of God's Creation concluded with this thought: "God saw all that He had made, and behold, IT WAS VERY GOOD." Now, some might say that God's work was completed when the sixth day of Creation was over, but you don't find anywhere that says, "And God saw that IT WAS COMPLETE." 4,000 years later, however, as Jesus was dying on the cross He uttered these famous words, "IT IS FINISHED!"

This is my conclusion about the matter: As good as God's Creation is and has been, Creation is incomplete until a man receives the redemption that is offered to him through Jesus' death on the cross. So, where are you in the Creation process today? Good, Very Good... or FINISHED?

Ephesians 2:10 (NAS)
For we are His workmanship, created in Christ Jesus for good works, which God prepared beforehand so that we would walk in them.

BE POSITIVE

Thanks to all of my math teachers who helped me throughout my school career. Because of you I continue to remember that POSITIVE is greater than NEGATIVE. I have to admit, though, that sometimes what you taught me has been challenged. There have been times that I've heard 3 positive things and just 1 negative thing, and the 1 negative seemed to affect me in a greater way than the positive. But that's when I go back to the basics you taught me in my early years. +3 will always and forever be greater than -1. And, with this in mind, I continue to remind myself, and others around me, that even though we live in a negative world I can change the equation by speaking positive in it, and that's what I will continue to do. After all, I have the GREATER ONE inside of me... I'm positive about that.

1 John 4:4 (KJV)
Greater is he that is in you, than he that is in the world.

TODAY'S FOOD FOR THOUGHT
The key to happiness is found under the Welcome Mat to God's House.

THE KIND OF PERSON GOD LIKES TO USE
May 2 | October 30

I was teaching a Bible Study on HOPE one night at a halfway house for recovering drug addicts. One young man didn't offer himself much hope for his future. Within a period of 5 minutes he had used the following words in association with himself: dirtbag, screw-up, idiot and laughing-stock. Since this was my first time to meet the young man, and since I had no idea what his life had been like up to this point, I could not deny any of his self accusations. Instead, I smiled at him and said, "You're the kind of person that God likes to use!" He looked at me with a puzzled expression so I explained, "People who think they've got it "all together" and take a lot of pride in their accomplishments usually have a hard time giving God the proper credit for what He does in their lives. But folks like you, who feel like they're "mess-ups" and don't have a lot to offer, have no problem giving God proper credit when He does great things in their lives because they realize what they are without Him. Yes... you're exactly the kind of person that God likes to use!"

1 Samuel 15:17 (NIV)
Samuel said, "Although you were once small in your own eyes, did you not become the head of the tribes of Israel? The LORD anointed you king over Israel."

STRENGTH

Philippians 4:13 (NAS)
I CAN DO all things through Him who STRENGTHENS me.

Notice the words in all caps in the scripture verse above? I'm putting emphasis there for an important reason. Christ most definitely is the supplier, but He gets things done by giving US STRENGTH so WE CAN DO what needs to be done. Too many times we're guilty of saying, "It's all up to the Lord!" If it truly is "all up to the Lord" then why would He need to give us STRENGTH? And why would we say "I CAN DO" if He is the One doing it? Meditate on this thought.

1 Corinthians 3:9 - "For we are labourers together with God"

TODAY'S FOOD FOR THOUGHT
A Message for Control Freaks: "Control Yourself!" (Galatians 5:23)

GROWING SPIRITUAL MUSCLE
May 3 | October 31

One of the main ways muscles grow is through tension. When muscle fibers undergo tension (like the tension experienced during resistance training) the muscle fiber becomes torn and damaged, and satellite cells come to aid in the repair of the damaged muscle fiber. Those cells connect to the damaged fiber and essentially repair the damaged muscles while at the same time adding bulk and strength to the muscle. So, the process goes like this:

1.) muscle fiber undergoes tension
2.) tension tears and damages muscle fiber
3.) satellite cells come to aid damaged fiber
4.) the addition of the new satellite cells increase muscle size and strength.

Isn't it interesting that tension is the catalyst that builds strength in the human body? The only difference between my muscles and those of Mr. Universe is that mine haven't gone through as much tension. Spiritual strength is achieved in much the same way as physical strength. People who undergo times of crisis and tension in their lives are on their way to gaining spiritual strength if they don't give up during those times of conflict. So, as much as we might enjoy the easy, carefree times of our lives just remember, it's during times of tension that our strength is increased. Just as our physical muscle is built quickly through "resistance training" our spiritual muscle is also built up during "resistance training." When the enemy attacks us we are encouraged to overcome him with these words, "RESIST the devil and he will flee from you" (James 4:7). RESISTANCE training... that's what we need to grow spiritual muscle!

Ephesians 6:10
Finally, my brethren, be strong in the Lord, and in the power of his might.

TODAY'S FOOD FOR THOUGHT

A small, plastic 5-gallon bucket full of water looked up at a large, 50-gallon steel drum and said "I sure do envy you! I wish I was as big, strong and impressive as you!" To which the steel drum replied, "But I am empty, and you are full... it is I who envy you!"
Moral of the story: Your container doesn't define you... your contents do.

SEEING THROUGH GOD'S EYES
May 4 | November 1

There was an elementary-aged boy in my class at church that was pushing every single one of my buttons. He was being extremely obnoxious, and I was having a difficult time getting his cooperation. When it was time for the Scripture lesson for the evening he continued with his antics and was being a major distraction as we read about Jesus healing a paralyzed man. When the story was over I asked the kids if they knew anybody that was similar to the paralyzed man in the story who might need our prayers. The hyperactive boy quieted down for a moment and raised his hand. I saw compassion in his eyes as he called out the name of two friends that he wanted us to pray for. All of my misgivings about the boy vanished in an instant. I hate to admit it, but up until that moment he had been an annoyance to me. But, then I saw the spirit of the boy... a caring, compassionate spirit. None of his negative attributes mattered to me anymore. After our prayer time, just a couple of minutes later, he was back to the rambunctious fellow that was pushing my buttons earlier... but he wasn't pushing my buttons anymore, because I was seeing him differently now.

Isn't that what we all need? A moment in time when we see people through different eyes... when we see the spirit within? Science says that human beings are nothing more than a very complex, highly evolved system of muscles, tissues, nerves, and chemicals. It's easy to get irritated at a person when you see them as just a bundled system of nerve endings that are getting on "your last nerve." But the Bible tells us in Job 32:8 "... there is a SPIRIT in man; and the inspiration of the Almighty giveth them understanding." Yes, there is something more to a person than what we see with our eyes. When we can get past all of the externals and see the spirit on the inside, and see the tender interior that gets overshadowed by a rough or obnoxious exterior, that's when we're seeing people through different eyes... that's when we're seeing through the eyes of God. "Lord open our eyes to see others the way you see them. Amen."

1 Samuel 16:7 (NAS)
"...for God sees not as man sees, for man looks at the outward appearance, but the LORD looks at the heart."

YOUR SMILE FOR TODAY
He who would like a promotion tomorrow should stop causing a commotion today. (Psalm 75:6-7)

LESSONS FROM THE PRODIGAL SON
May 5 | November 2

There are a few things that I know about God (and about us) simply by reading the story of the Prodigal Son found in Luke 15. Here goes:

1. You can be living in the Father's House and be dissatisfied and discontented to the point where you think you're missing out on something and want to leave.
2. The Father will let you leave His House and presence so you can follow a meaningless pursuit.
3. When you leave the Father's House, you leave His presence. His presence is "where He is." To have the relationship restored YOU must return to HIM.
4. There is a certain amount of fun and pleasure that a person can obtain in the world, outside of the Father's House.
5. Any fun or pleasure that can be achieved outside of the Father's House will eventually end and the person who once lived in the Father's House will realize that things weren't so bad in the Father's House after all. (It's called "coming to your senses.")
6. People who have left the Father's House to pursue an ungodly lifestyle will feel a sense of shame and unworthiness for their error and will be doubtful within themselves that the Father will accept them back into the family.
7. If/when you return to the Father's House, He will receive you back with open arms and will remove your feelings of unworthiness.
8. If you return back to the Father, He will restore your broken relationship with Him, EVEN THOUGH others may disapprove of the restoration. (Remember the older son?)
9. When you are away from the Father's House, He considers you to be LOST and DEAD... when you return He considers you to be FOUND and ALIVE. (This story lets us know that there is a deeper meaning to the word "DEAD" than what we have imagined.)
10. The Father loves you. Even though you left Him, you can return to Him... if you will "come to your senses."

Luke 15:17 (NIV)
When he came to his senses, he said, 'How many of my father's hired servants have food to spare, and here I am starving to death!

MAKE A MINOR TWEAK!
May 6 | November 3

With just the smallest tweak, the negative word "complaint" becomes the positive word "compliant." Just move the "i" and the "a" around and you go from being "the voice of discontent" to being "the agreeable one." That's the way it is with life. Some folks think you've got to go on some great spiritual pilgrimage to discover the good and the positive that's out there. In reality, just a simple tweak in attitude and perspective can change everything. Today, when you sense a complaint rising up within you, but you haven't let it out yet, just make a minor tweak. Find something to be thankful for and release that out of your mouth instead, and watch the negative situation turn into a positive one.

1 Thessalonians 5:18 (NAS)
In everything give thanks; for this is God's will for you in Christ Jesus.

PERSISTENCE

Maybe you've heard this modern-day definition for INSANITY: "To do the same thing over and over again, while expecting different results." Did you know that is also the definition for PERSISTENCE? Persistence is rarely found in people today (maybe because it has the same definition as INSANITY). What marathon runner gives up at the 20 mile mark just because he's been doing "the same thing" without getting different results? The results a marathon runner is looking for is at the 26 mile mark – the Finish Line. It doesn't matter to him that he's been doing the same thing over and over again… one foot in front of the other, sweat dripping, heart pounding, mile-after-mile tediousness. The Finish Line is the desired result and it will not be achieved any other way than by "doing the same thing over and over again." Friends, life is like a race, and it's not a 100 yard dash. It's a marathon. Many times you have to keep on doing the same thing over and over again because that's exactly what's needed to achieve the desired results. It may sound like INSANITY to some… sounds like PERSISTENCE to me.

Matthew 24:13 (KJV)
But he that shall endure unto the end, the same shall be saved.

TODAY'S FOOD FOR THOUGHT
When you're feeling empty, a great place to be is right next to somebody whose cup is overflowing.

THE APPOINTED ONE
May 7 | November 4

I was teaching my elementary kids at church about Bible names and their meanings. I shared a list of about 15 names. 3 of the names mentioned were names of kids that were in my group... Ethan, Matthew, and Seth. Ethan means "solid, enduring," Matthew means "gift of God" and Seth means "appointed." Seth laughed when I told him what his name meant. I don't think he grasped what the word "appointed" meant, so as I tried to define the word for him a strange unction came upon me to speak a word of encouragement to him concerning his future. I laid my hand upon his shoulder and said, "You have a purpose and a destiny... you are appointed by God to fulfill a mission... You will be used by God and be useful to Him... nothing about your life will be wasted because you are SETH THE APPOINTED ONE."

Have you ever been in a moment in time when you felt like a life-changing experience took place but nobody around you even noticed it? That night was such a moment for this little boy, I believe. I don't know all of the things that have been spoken to this boy in the past... critical, negative words concerning his character or future... but I sensed that his destiny was brightened by the words God gave me to speak to him. It doesn't matter to me if he remembers me in the future or if he remembers that moment in time when I spoke those words to him. What matters is that he becomes the man God said he would be... SETH THE APPOINTED ONE.

This is a part of children's ministry that you don't hear about much. It's not just babysitting kids while the adults get the "real" ministry. It's speaking into young lives and giving them a word about themselves that they will hopefully carry with them all their days. That's why I love children's ministry and will keep on doing it, most likely, until the day I die.

Matthew 19:13 (NIV)
Then people brought little children to Jesus for him to place his hands on them and pray for them.

TODAY'S WORD OF EXHORTATION
You don't need to feel *pressured*, but you do need to feel *challenged*. Pressure comes from the outside, from opposing forces. Challenge comes from within the spirit of a man who knows he can achieve more than he's currently achieving. Having difficulties? Accept the challenge!

WHEN I DIE
May 8 | November 5

I used to say, along with most other folks I know, "When I die I want to go peacefully in my sleep." Now, I'm not planning on dying any time soon, but recently I've changed my philosophy. When I die I don't want to go in my sleep. No! I want to go while I'm actively doing something. I want to go while I'm playing the guitar and leading worship. I want to go while I'm playing dodge-ball with my elementary kids at church (Morbid thought, I know, but hear me out). I want to go while I'm on my morning prayer walk. I want to go while working on a job for one of my customers. I want to go while I'm leading a Bible Study at the Men's Home. Yes! I want to go while I'm doing something... especially if it's something for God's kingdom!

How did Jesus "die?" He died with an audience in front of Him. He died giving of himself. He died with a goal in mind. He died pressing toward God's will. Even when He was on the cross dying for our sins he was still ministering to others. (Remember the thief?) He is my example.

I definitely don't want to die while laying down on the couch eating Little Debbie Swiss Rolls and watching another episode of Seinfeld. If I want my life to count, I want my death to count also. I want to die having squeezed every ounce of purpose out of this life that God had for me.

Perhaps this is a morbid thought to some, but maybe it's just the kind of thinking that could lead us toward making each moment count more before our time comes. No, I don't want to leave this world on a downward slope... I want to leave it while climbing a mountain!

Romans 14:8 (NAS)
For if we live, we live for the Lord, or if we die, we die for the Lord; therefore whether we live or die, we are the Lord's.

YOUR SMILE FOR TODAY
Isn't it interesting how people measure their success by the amount of "stuff" they accumulate in life. They have a pile of awards, a pile of material possessions and a pile of money. Then they measure their piles against other people's piles to see who was more successful. The one with the biggest (and most) piles wins. Cows measure their success in a similar way.

GIVE ME THE BAD NEWS FIRST
May 9 | November 6

A friend called me the other day and said, "I've got good news, and I've got bad news." I said, "Give me the bad news first" and he did. After the bad news was out of the way all of my angst, and any fear that I might have had, was gone because I knew the good news was all that was left. Then he told me the good news, and it overshadowed the impact of the bad news. That's just the way I like it. What about you? Maybe I unwittingly picked up this life philosophy from the Bible. After all, the Bible starts off with the bad news first.

THE BAD NEWS:
The bad news is that man sinned and got separated from God. The bad news is that the world plummeted into a state of disorder because of a curse. The bad news is that even though man tried to find his way back to God he continually fell short. Disease, despair and slavery are recorded on a regular basis as a result.

Yes, the Old Testament is like God telling us "The Bad News First". He got it all out of the way up front. But then came "The Good News". The news that you and I are the recipients of. The good news is the New Testament.

THE GOOD NEWS:
The good news is that God so loved the world that He gave His only Son. The good news is that all of our sins are washed away by confessing the Lordship of Jesus. The good news is that we are forgiven. The good news is that health can be restored through God's gift of healing. The good news is that we can receive eternal and abundant life. The good news is that everything that's been stolen and lost can be restored back to us.

All the bad news has been overshadowed by this good news! Don't you like getting the good news last?!

Luke 8:1 (NIV)
After this, Jesus traveled about from one town and village to another, proclaiming the GOOD NEWS of the kingdom of God.

TODAY'S FOOD FOR THOUGHT
Some people's words are like water to a thirsty soul.
Other people's words are like water to a drowning soul.
"Death and Life are in the power of the tongue." Proverbs 18:21.

EXTRA-ORDINARY
May 10 | November 7

A miraculous event happened in the life of a man named Cornelius. An angel appeared to him and told him to send some men to get the Apostle Peter and bring him to his house. Cornelius did as the angel instructed, and Peter came and preached to Cornelius and his family, and they were all saved as a result (Acts 10).

Now, here's a question: Which event would be more fantastic, more memorable, more earth-shaking to you... a visitation from an angel, or a visitation from a preacher who had a message of eternal significance? Which of these two events is the real "miraculous event"? The EXTRAORDINARY visit from the perfect, heavenly angel, or the ORDINARY visit from the earthly preacher... the man made of flesh... riddled with imperfections... the man who 3 times denied he knew Jesus? It was the message from the ORDINARY man that changed Cornelius' life and altered his eternal destiny, not the EXTRAORDINARY visitation from the angel. So, remember this: in your pursuit of an EXTRAORDINARY God don't overlook the ORDINARY people He uses... and the EXTRAORDINARY message that they deliver.

STRENGTH

Thought for Today: You have a part to play in the fulfillment of God's plan for your life. It's not "all up to God." How do we know this? Nehemiah 8:10 says, "The joy of the Lord is your STRENGTH." Isaiah 40:31 says, "They that wait upon the Lord shall renew their STRENGTH." Philippians 4:13 says, "I can do all things through Christ who gives me STRENGTH." All three of these verses mention the word STRENGTH. So, what is strength needed for? It's needed in order to do a job or to accomplish something. Why would WE need strength if God is the One doing everything? Think about it. There is a purpose and plan for your life... ask God to give you the STRENGTH you need to fulfill it!

1 Corinthians 3:9
For we are labourers together with God

TODAY'S FOOD FOR THOUGHT
If you're trying to put the pieces of your life together and they don't seem to fit maybe you don't have all of the pieces yet. (Romans 8:28)

NO SLEEP DISORDER HERE!
May 11 | November 8

I think it's interesting, and not at all coincidental, that the only record we have of Jesus sleeping is when he slept in the back of the boat during a violent storm... a storm that the disciples thought would cause their death. Wind blowing, waves crashing, boat filling with water and being tossed to and fro - and Jesus sleeping like a baby through it all.

As I watch the television and see all of the products on the market today for sleeping disorders I think that maybe Jesus has a secret to sleep that we all need to know about. A secret that not only helps a person sleep when the going is good, but also when we're facing critical moments that seem like "life or death." Yes, if He could sleep with waves splashing in his face, wind howling, boat rocking, and the sounds of grown men crying out in fear, I think you could say that He is an "authority on sleep."

So what is this secret to peaceful sleep that Jesus experienced? Perhaps the answer comes directly from His mouth after he calmed the storm with the command "Peace, be still" then looked to his disciples and said, "Why is it that you have NO FAITH?"

Faith – a simple trust that everything is in God's Hands, including you and me. Faith – the belief that everything is "working together for good" to those who love God and are called according to His purpose. Faith – the ability to see past the current set of circumstances by taking hold of God's promises of provision and protection. Faith – it's an amazing sleep aid!

Proverbs 3:24 (KJV)
When thou liest down, thou shalt not be afraid: yea, thou shalt lie down, and thy sleep shall be sweet.
Psalm 127:2 (NIV)
In vain you rise early and stay up late, toiling for food to eat-- for he grants sleep to those he loves.

TODAY'S WORD OF ENCOURAGEMENT

Two of my favorite Bible verses are: *"Greater is He that is in you than he that is in the world"* (1 John 4:4) and, *"I can do all things through Christ who gives me strength."* (Philippians 4:13)
Mesh these two verses together and you get something like this:
"'The One inside you that says 'You Can Do It' is greater than the one in the world that says 'You Can't.'"

JINXES
May 12 | November 9

Do you believe in Jinxes? Basically, when you get down to brass tacks, a "jinx" is a belief that you can curse a good situation by saying something GOOD about it. If you landed the best job of your life and then say, "This is going to be the best job ever" those words could become a jinx (a curse) that will turn the good situation into bad. Now, many don't think twice about saying something BAD about a GOOD situation, and don't consider it a curse at all. Things like: "Things are good now, but I'm just waiting for the other shoe to drop"... "I'm sure this good fortune won't last"... "Nothing ever goes my way." We even say that a person is being "humble" for doing so. Yet, if you get excited about a good situation, and feel hopeful about the future you can't speak GOOD about it for fear that you might JINX it. Let me get this straight... you can say something BAD about your GOOD situation and that's okay, but you can't say something GOOD about it or you'll probably jinx it? That kind of thinking doesn't make good sense, and it's obviously our enemy who wants us to think that way.

What kind of life is it that God has given us that we can't be confident about our future, that we can't speak good (a blessing) about our situation, that we can't have expectations that things will go our way and in our favor simply because we're His children? Only the Devil would try to convince us that we shouldn't speak good about our situation. He knows too well that when we speak "good" we pronounce a blessing and that we're speaking in faith... that God can add His anointing to those positive, faith-filled words. Don't be duped by the Devil into believing you've got to be a lowly, self-deprecating individual, unworthy of good things happening for you. So, here's a refresher course.... when you speak good about your good situation it's not called a JINX it's called a BLESSING... when you speak bad about it, that's called a CURSE!

Psalm 109:17
As he loved cursing, so let it come unto him: as he delighted not in blessing, so let it be far from him.

TODAY'S FOOD FOR THOUGHT
A wonderful freedom is FOUND
when the fear of what others think is LOST.
*"The fear of man brings a snare,
But he who trusts in the LORD will be exalted." Proverbs 29:25*

MILK AND HONEY
May 13 | November 10

You've probably heard this phrase associated with the Promised Land: *"A land flowing with milk and honey."* Sounds like a good place to live! But, just understand this… if it's flowing with milk and honey then you better be willing to milk some cows… and you better get over your fear of being stung by bees! Yes, even in the Promised Land there's work to be done. Honey doesn't flow from the hive into a quart jar on the breakfast table, and milk doesn't flow from a cow's udder into a gallon jug in your refrigerator. God has awesome blessings available for you in the Promised Land, but you may need to roll your sleeves up to receive them (or in the case of harvesting honey from a bee hive, roll your sleeves down).

FLAWED HUMANS

Think about the people that Jesus chose to be his disciples. Matthew was a tax collector who was hated by the Jews because he worked for the Roman government. Peter was a "big-talker," but in the end he denied that he even knew Jesus. Judas, well, you know his story… betrayer. James and John? They wanted to call down fire from Heaven on a village that rejected Jesus (now there's some Christian love at work for you). And who can forget Thomas… the doubter. I've just named 6 of Jesus' 12 disciples. That's half of the group, and all of these guys had some pretty obvious flaws in their character or attitudes. So, what's my point? God likes to use flawed humans… mostly because that's the only kind there are. And you thought God wouldn't be able to use you! HA!

1 Corinthians 1:26-29 (NAS)
For consider your calling, brethren, that there were not many wise according to the flesh, not many mighty, not many noble ; but God has chosen the foolish things of the world to shame the wise, and God has chosen the weak things of the world to shame the things which are strong, and the base things of the world and the despised God has chosen, the things that are not, so that He may nullify the things that are, so that no man may boast before God.

TODAY'S WISDOM NUGGET
The goal of true wisdom is to win souls… not arguments.
"The fruit of the righteous is a tree of life,
and he who wins souls is WISE." Proverbs 11:30

YOUR TRUE VALUE
May 14 | November 11

An acquaintance of mine sold 4 very old silver dollars for $20 a piece at an auction I went to. When I asked him about the coins he said, "Those were my wife's coins. Do you know where she got them from?" He went on to tell me that his wife works in a restaurant in Cullman and that one of her customers had a ticket for $4. He had no other money on him at the time so he paid his bill with the 4 old silver dollars... 4 silver dollars that someone paid $80 for just a few days later at the auction. I was stunned. All four coins have the inscription written on the back "ONE DOLLAR" so the man had every right to legally pay his bill with the currency, but he obviously did not realize the true value of the coins.

What made those ONE DOLLAR coins so valuable? 2 things: Their content (silver) and their age (historical/antique value). Many folks today are much like those old coins at the auction. They have been given a label by society, government, business, church, etc., and that label has given them their designation of their own personal value. They carry their value with them everywhere they go much like those silver coins carry "ONE DOLLAR" on their backs. Unfortunately, the label does not tell two important things about the person: their content (what they're made of) or their historical value (due to their life experiences). If you think you're "past your prime" and are diminishing in value I'd like to contradict that thought. Your content and your accumulated experiences in life have made you more valuable than what your man-made label denotes. Others may not see it and may mistakenly sell you short of your true value, much like the man who surrendered his valuable coins to pay for a $4 meal. But your true value is greater than you've possibly ever imagined.... just consider the price that God paid for you:

For you know that God paid a ransom to save you from the empty life you inherited from your ancestors. And the ransom he paid was not mere gold or silver. He paid for you with the precious lifeblood of Christ, the sinless, spotless Lamb of God.
1 Peter 1:18-19 (NLT)

TODAY'S WISDOM NUGGET
Let this determination be in you: "If the devil wants to curse me he'll have to use somebody else's mouth... not mine!" Don't be an unwitting participant in cursing your own life. Speak blessings over yourself!

HOLY
May 15 | November 12

I just can't get away from the thought that there is a REALLY important reason why angels circle God's throne day and night and continually repeat "Holy, Holy, Holy is the Lord God Almighty" without ceasing, throughout eternity. Think of all the words that describe God that could be spoken and repeated around His throne. It could have been "Love, Love, Love is the Lord God Almighty" or "Powerful, Powerful, Powerful is the Lord God Almighty" or "Merciful, Merciful, Merciful is the Lord God Almighty" or even "Joy, Joy, Joy is the Lord God Almighty." But, instead the word "HOLY" is used… a word that is so appropriate and fitting and accurate in describing God's character that it is eternally spoken around His throne. And, the fact that it is spoken without ceasing tells me something else… that somehow this word "HOLY" has more meaning in Heaven than it has here on Earth. How easily we would tire and grow bored of continually saying "Holy, Holy, Holy is the Lord God Almighty" in a worship service here on Earth (for even the short span of one hour). But, there is no boredom in Heaven and new meaning of His holiness is extracted each time the word is spoken. It does not become redundant, but instead, new revelation of God's holiness is unveiled each time it is spoken, so that those speaking it never tire in saying it and repeating it.

Oh, that we on Earth could get even the smallest revelation of what that word HOLY means. Perhaps we would not be so quick to hold on to our pet sins, our complaints and our unforgiveness if we understood what HOLY means. Perhaps we would fight with greater fervency when tempted by the wicked one to succumb to the lusts of our flesh if we fully grasped God's holiness. But, alas, we are here on Earth where we "see through a glass darkly" and a veil covers our eyes to the great revelation of this one word that best describes our God in Heaven…… HOLY.

Revelation 4:8
And they rest not day and night, saying, Holy, holy, holy, Lord God Almighty, which was, and is, and is to come.

TODAY'S WISDOM NUGGET
In the word "unclear" if you switch the first two letters around you get "nuclear". But just because things look "unclear" doesn't mean you're in for an explosion! It's just another opportunity to walk by faith.
"For we walk by faith, not by sight." 2 Cor. 5:7

DON'T BE "DUMB"

May 16 | November 13

Sometimes we just don't realize how the words we say can mess up the answer to our prayers. Take Zacharias for instance. The angel Gabriel came to him and told him that his prayer had been heard and that he and his barren wife, Elizabeth, would have a son... the son they longed for and prayed for. Zacharias was overwhelmed by this information and with doubt-filled words said, "How can this be since I'm an old man and my wife is well-striken in years?" In response to his doubt concerning the answer to his prayers Zacharias was struck dumb (unable to speak) for a season of time until his baby, John, was born. Can I suggest that maybe, just maybe, he was struck dumb (unable to speak) so that his doubt-filled words wouldn't derail the blessing that was on its way?

Today, unfortunately, miraculous interventions like this don't take place often when we speak doubt-filled words in regards to the answers to our prayers. Maybe you've prayed for a financial blessing to come your way, but you've been saying, "I guess I'll always be broke!" Or maybe you've prayed for healing in your body, but you've been saying, "I'll never get over this sickness!" Perhaps you've prayed for a change in your circumstances, but you continue to say, "Nothing ever goes my way!" These kinds of doubt-filled words negate the faith-filled prayers that you pray.

Yes, God will let us talk ourselves right out of the blessing that He wants to give us. An angel won't come and strike us dumb when we start "speaking doubt." But, make no mistake... we're definitely being "dumb" when we speak words of doubt concerning God's answers to our prayers!

My Prayer for Today: "Lord, keep my mouth from saying words that hinder Your answers to my prayers! In Jesus' name I pray. Amen."

Luke 1:20
And, behold, thou shalt be dumb, and not able to speak, until the day that these things shall be performed, because thou believest not my words, which shall be fulfilled in their season.

TODAY'S WISDOM NUGGET

A carrier of the rhinovirus (the common cold) will not infect others with the germ as long as he keeps his mouth shut. But when he OPENS HIS MOUTH to sneeze or cough the infection spreads. Bad attitudes are spread in much the same way.

STRONGER THAN YOU THINK
May 17 | November 14

You are stronger than you think. You can go farther than you think. You can hang on longer than you think. How do I know this? Because I've done all three. The very first time this revelation hit me was when I was running a race in college during our intramural Olympics. It was an 800 meter (1/2 mile) race… two laps around the track. I led the pack for the first lap of the race and the closest runner to me was at least 50 feet behind me. But somewhere around the 600 meter mark my "engines" started failing. The pack began to close in on me and somewhere around the final curve of the last lap an opponent passed me in a full sprint. I thought in my mind, "Well, I gave it my best shot but I'm not winning today." But then, from somewhere deep inside of me, I found another gear that I had never used before. We were on the straightaway headed toward the finish line and I could see the runner who passed me out in the lead by about 10 yards. I pulled out all the stops and sprinted, even though moments earlier I thought I had nothing left in me. In the final 30 yards of the race I overtook the guy who passed me and inched him out at the finish line. I won the race and discovered that I had more in me than I had previously thought.

You don't realize how much you have in you until it's put to the test. You can't find out if you're an overcomer unless there is something to overcome. So today I suggest that you accept the challenges that lay before you and don't give in to that doubting voice within that tells you "give up" or "settle for second place." There's a prize to be won and only those who step out of their comfort zone and press beyond their own limitations will discover it. When you press beyond your own limitations and find that "second gear" that's when you are trusting in something (and Someone) other than your own ability. That's where God's GRACE kicks in.

Philippians 3:13-14
Forgetting those things which are behind, and reaching forth unto those things which are before, I PRESS toward the mark for the PRIZE of the high calling of God in Christ Jesus.

TODAY'S WISDOM NUGGET
People who question other people's motivation usually have questionable motivation themselves. *"To the pure, all things are pure, but to those who are corrupted and do not believe, nothing is pure." Titus 1:15*

THINGS
May 18 | November 15

Here are a few thoughts about "THINGS:"

A. The Bible says God "richly supplies us with all THINGS to enjoy" (1 Timothy 6:17). Now, I'm no rocket scientist but here are a couple of things that I can deduce from this verse:

 1. God supplies us with THINGS.
 2. The THINGS are for our enjoyment.

B. The Bible also says, "Seek first the kingdom of God and His righteousness and all these THINGS shall be added unto you." (Matthew 6:33). Again, I'm no rocket scientist but here's what I deduce from this verse:

 1. If you're seeking God, he will give you THINGS.
 2. THINGS will be ADDED to you (not taken away) when you're serving God.

I don't see how people can get confused about this. Many "religious" people think that God doesn't want you to have THINGS. They think THINGS will stand in the way between you and God. But, if you're doing things God's way:

 1.) THINGS will be added to you, and,
 2.) God will supply THINGS simply for your enjoyment.

My Prayer for Today:
"Lord, you know the THINGS that I need in my life. I put You and Your kingdom first in my life, and trust that all the THINGS I need will be taken care of today."

Psalm 34:10 (NAS)
The young lions do lack and suffer hunger; But they who seek the LORD shall not be in want of any good THING.

TODAY'S WISDOM NUGGET
Don't waste time thinking about who is against you. Instead, think about who is for you. *"If God be for us, who can be against us?"* *Romans 8:31. "This I know, that God is for me." Psalm 56:9.*

144

SIX SIMPLE PHRASES
May 19 | November 16

There are six simple phrases I often encourage myself with when I'm experiencing a problem or going through difficulties.

1. DON'T GIVE UP!
"Let's not get tired of doing good, because in time we'll have a harvest if we don't give up."
Galatians 6:9

2. THERE'S A PRIZE AWAITING!
"Do you not know that those who run in a race all run, but only one receives the prize? Run in such a way that you may win." 1 Corinthians 9:24

3. GOD IS WATCHING ME.
"For the eyes of the LORD move to and fro throughout the earth that He may strongly support those whose heart is completely His."
2 Chronicles 16:9

4. GOD IS FOR ME!
"If God is for us who can be against us."
Romans 8:31

5. EVERYTHING WILL WORK OUT FOR MY GOOD.
"And we know that all things work together for good to those who love God, to those who are called according to His purpose."
Romans 8:28

6. THIS IS ONLY TEMPORARY.
"For momentary, light affliction is producing for us an eternal weight of glory far beyond all comparison."
2 Corinthians 4:17

1 Samuel 30:6
And David was greatly distressed... but David ENCOURAGED HIMSELF in the LORD his God.

TODAY'S WISDOM NUGGET
EQUAL OPPORTUNITY FAITH:
When you think about how big your God is at least as much as you think about how big your problems are.

GOD'S NOT INTERESTED IN NUMBERS?
May 20 | November 17

I've heard some people say, "God's not interested in numbers." I hate to be disagreeable, but I must insist that's not true. Here are 3 numbers that I'm positive God is interested in, because Jesus said it Himself:

ONE:

"I say unto you, that likewise joy shall be in heaven over ONE sinner that repents" Luke 15:7. (Jesus said that He would leave 99 sheep that are safe to go after just ONE that is lost... and Heaven rejoices when just ONE lost sinner is found!)

TWO:

"Again I say unto you, That if TWO of you shall agree on earth as touching any thing that they shall ask, it shall be done for them of my Father which is in heaven" Matthew 18:19. (Effectiveness in prayer doesn't come by having great numbers of people praying for/with you... it can come from just TWO who are in faith-filled AGREEMENT.

THREE:

"For where two or THREE are gathered together in my name, there am I in the midst of them" Matthew 18:20. (The world determines the success of an event based on how many people show up... but, we should determine the success of an event on whether or not Jesus shows up... it only takes TWO or THREE gathered in His name for this to happen.)

So you see, He really is interested in numbers... they just don't have to be BIG numbers. That should make someONE like you very happy!

Luke 15:4 (NIV)
"Suppose one of you has a hundred sheep and loses ONE of them. Doesn't he leave the ninety-nine in the open country and go after the lost sheep until he finds it?"

TODAY'S WISDOM NUGGET
Two of the hardest things you'll ever do:
1.) Be silent when you really want to say something.
2.) Say something when you really want to be silent.

AN INCONVENIENT DISTURBANCE
May 21 | November 18

The preacher asked all the kids to sit by me on the front row one Sunday morning at church. One little boy, who was having a difficult time sitting still and being quiet, sat right beside me. He wanted to talk to me but I was trying to turn his direction toward the preacher (after all that's what you're supposed to do in church). He finally calmed down and focused on what the preacher was saying.

The preacher mentioned the name "Timothy" in his sermon, and that seemed to activate the little boys "talk" button again. He leaned over to me and said (in a much louder voice than a whisper) "I have a friend at school…" but I interrupted, index finger pressed firmly against my lips, and said, "Shhh… pay attention to the preacher." But, he kept going, "He was different from the other kids at school. He got sick…." Again, I interrupted his story with, "Tell me about this after church… you need to listen to the preacher right now." (I was getting a little perturbed). But, he was relentless and continued, "He DIED last week. Every time the preacher says "Timothy" it makes me sad… 'cause that was his name." My heart sank as I realized that I was trying to "shush" something that really needed to be "let out."

All of the sudden the sermon didn't matter anymore… church "protocol" didn't matter anymore… an inconvenient disturbance didn't matter anymore. All that mattered was the heart of a little boy who missed his friend from school. A little boy who was looking to a grown man for some compassion. I quickly repented of my earlier cold response to him and then laid my hand upon his hand and looked into his eyes, and whispered "I'm so sorry, buddy." Holding on to his hand, I prayed for him under my breath as the preacher continued with his sermon. I realized that what had just transpired with the little boy was just as important than the words coming from the pulpit. God spoke to me through that little boy about showing compassion even when it's seemingly "out-of-place" and inconvenient.

One day I may forget the words spoken by the preacher that Sunday morning, but I'll never forget the sermon God spoke to me through the little boy on the front row of that church.

My Prayer for Today: "Lord, help me open my eyes to the needs of others around me and to always be prepared to help and serve… even when it's seemingly inconvenient and out-of-place. Amen."

BIBLE DIRECTION
May 22 | November 19

Several years ago I was presented with an opportunity that would most definitely change the course and direction of my life. I had never been good at making decisions, and this one was one of the biggest of my life. The decision required me moving my little family halfway across the country. I only had a couple of months to decide. I had sought the counsel of others (friends, relatives, etc.) but everything seemed foggy to me. One night, as I was studying a Bible lesson for an upcoming children's Bible study, I was reading the story of "Peter Walking on the Water" and the answer came to me in an instant. As I read how Peter stepped out of the comfort of his fishing boat to join Jesus walking on the water I realized that I, too, had to leave my comfort zone and step out into the unknown. I received direction for my life that night just by reading a simple story from the Bible… and I'm certain I made the right decision.

God's Word is good like that. Psalms 119:105 says, "Your word is a lamp unto my feet and a light unto my path." Sometimes we just don't know what our next steps should be. We look to others for advice and counsel. We call friends and relatives and ask them what they would do in our situation. Although all of these avenues for direction are viable, can I suggest that we go to the Operator's Manual and see what our Creator says? So many times I've read the Bible and gotten answers to my questions and direction for my journey simply from reading simple stories of those who have gone on before me. The Bible stories aren't fiction… they are actual accounts of men and women who needed God's help and direction… and He supplied them with their answer. I've always heard that we should "listen to the voice of experience." The Bible is full of people whose experiences are written down for us to learn from and to follow.

So, for those who are wondering what their next steps in life should be, before you go ask everyone else what their advice and opinion is, I'd like to recommend a really good book to you.

Psalm 119:133 (NIV) "Direct my footsteps according to your word"

TODAY'S WORD OF EXHORTATION
DETERMINATION: a fixed movement or tendency toward an object or end. Firmness of purpose; resolve. Be a person of determination!

NO LOOKING BACK
May 23 | November 20

I guess I was about 19 years old when I had my very first "fender-bender." I had just gotten a roast beef sandwich at the Arby's drive-through and was waiting to merge on to Sixth Avenue as I sat behind another car. I looked over my shoulder and there were no cars coming in our direction. The car ahead of me began to pull out on to Sixth Avenue. He had pulled out about 5-10 feet and was accelerating, so all signs led me to believe that he was merging on to the highway. Seeing that he was moving forward, I let off my brake and slowly began to accelerate, taking another glance over my shoulder to make sure no cars were coming. In that split second, while I was looking over my shoulder, the driver ahead of me put on his brakes for some unexplained reason and I ran right into him. Luckily for me, there was no major damage done and the driver of the other car was very understanding and forgiving.

It was on that day that I learned the importance of keeping my eyes ahead of me while accelerating. MOVING FORWARD WHILE LOOKING BACKWARD is a very dangerous proposition. Jesus said, "No man having put his hand to the plow and looking back is fit for the kingdom of God" (Luke 9:62). He had a very good reason for saying this.

We all have both good things and bad things in our past that we look back on (either affectionately, or with remorse.) It's safe to look back when your foot is on the brake... when you've stopped for a moment to reflect on what you did right or wrong... when you've stopped and can make the necessary adjustments to your life. But as soon as you decide to move on, to move forward, there can be no looking backward. It is unsafe. It can even be dangerous. Yes, there is a very good reason why the Bible says, "Forgetting what lies behind and reaching forward to what lies ahead"... it's the SAFEST way to live.

Philippians 3:13
This one thing I do, forgetting those things which are behind, and reaching forth unto those things which are before.

TODAY'S WORD OF ENCOURAGEMENT
"A cheerful heart has a continual feast." Proverbs 15:15.
Cheer up... and chow down!

FLY

May 24 | November 21

I was inspired to write this little poem after watching a baby Robin testing out her wings one spring morning:

Baby Robin in her nest.
Mom pushed her out, it's for the best,
And thus begins her biggest test.
Will she fly like all the rest?

While in the nest her feathers grew,
And her wings developed, too,
But these are things she never knew,
Up until the day she FLEW.

And some of us are like that bird.
All through our lives we have heard,
"You can fly!" It seemed absurd.
So, we just ignored that word.

And God must push us from our nest,
From our comfort, ease and rest.
He does it so that we'll be blessed,
And reach new levels on our quest.

Don't be surprised, don't question "Why?"
When you meet Challenge eye-to-eye,
God has a plan, don't whine or cry,
He pushed your from your nest…TO FLY!

Isaiah 40:31
But they that wait upon the LORD shall renew their strength; they shall mount up with wings as eagles; they shall run, and not be weary; and they shall walk, and not faint.

TODAY'S WISDOM NUGGET

There are no 5 ft. tall centers in the NBA, nor are there any 7 ft. tall jockeys at the Kentucky Derby. It's been wrongly said "You can be anything you want to be!" A more accurate statement is "You can discover what God has made you to be… and be that."
"We are His workmanship." Eph 2:10

VISION AND RESTRAINT
May 25 | November 22

Proverbs 29:18 says, "Where there is no vision the people perish." I like the way the American Standard Version puts it… "Where there is no vision, the people cast off restraint." Think about what VISION means, and what RESTRAINT means. VISION, to put it simply, is "a picture you can see in your mind concerning your future." A very simple definition for RESTRAINT is "the ability to control one's own actions and to say 'NO' to harmful desires." Putting these two simple definitions together, here's what Proverbs is saying: "When people can't get a picture in their mind about who they will be in their future, they will refuse to say 'NO' to harmful desires and actions in their present."

When you're at the local buffet and you refuse to show restraint, you will go through the line a third and fourth time because you don't have a vision of yourself in the future… in this case a future where you will most likely be overweight. The young man or woman that is strolling through the department store and refuses to restrain themselves may decide to shoplift. They do so because they have no vision of their future… in this case a future life of jail time and possibly even prison time. The teenagers that won't say "NO" to drugs and alcohol do so because they don't have a vision of their future… a future filled with addiction, rehab, family problems, etc.

Many times we focus on people's problems and tell them, "Stop Overeating! Stop Stealing! Stop Using Drugs!" People can't stop themselves when they're in the middle of these things. Not unless they can get a vision of their future… unless they can see down the road they're currently on… unless they can get a picture in their mind of who they will be a couple of years from now if they don't stop.

If you're dealing with a person who has addictive behaviors, keep praying for them. But, also encourage them to get a VISION for their future. A VISION of what their life will be like if they don't stop… if they keep on the path of destructive behavior they're on. But, also encourage them to get a vision of the person they want to become. If they can get a VISION of themselves having a happy, prosperous and successful future maybe that VISION will help them restrain themselves in the present.

Proverbs 25:28 (ASV)
He whose spirit is without restraint is like a city that is broken down and without walls.

PAST MY PRIME
May 26 | November 23

The other day somebody told me I was "past my prime." I wasn't sure what they meant… it sounded like an insult, but I thought I'd look up the word PRIME in the dictionary just to find out what the definition is. I'm so glad I did!

I found out that, in painting, when you PRIME something you are putting an undercoat of paint on the surface to cover defects and flaws so that the final, lasting coat of paint can be applied. I also found out that when you PRIME an engine you are getting gas to it so that it can start easily and run smoothly. Last, but not least, I also discovered that, in mathematics, PRIME numbers are numbers that are only divisible by themselves and by the number one.

After putting all of this information together I realized that person was not insulting me (wink, wink)… they were complementing me!

You see, I am no longer showing an undercoat of paint that simply hides all of my faults and defects, because I AM PAST MY PRIME. I have my final coat of paint on that shows my lasting and true colors.

I no longer have need of people pumping gas to my engine to try and get me up and running, because I AM PAST MY PRIME. My engine is finally running smoothly and efficiently with little need for "cheerleaders and superficial motivators."

And, finally, I am no longer a number whose sole interest is in itself, who has made itself #1, because I AM PAST MY PRIME. I care about a number of others whose lives I try to enrich and encourage by intermingling my interests with theirs.

Yes, I am past my prime, and it feels good. Are you past your prime yet?

Psalm 92:14 (NIV)
They will still bear fruit in old age, they will stay fresh and green.

TODAY'S WISDOM NUGGET
God is the SMARTEST and most POWERFUL Being there is, yet He is best known for His LOVE. What are you striving to be known for?
Brains, Muscles… or Heart?

WHAT HAVE YOU BEEN THINKING?
May 27 | November 24

I was driving by myself in my truck one morning and I thought about something funny a guy told me the previous night... I laughed out loud! Forgive me for being hyper-analytical about this, but isn't it interesting that you can THINK about something funny and it will make you laugh out loud, and you can THINK about something "happy" and it can make you smile, and you can THINK about something sad, depressing or negative and it can make you frown?

Truth is, you can tell a lot about what people are THINKING just by their countenance... they don't even have to say a word. What have you been THINKING about? Most likely your facial expressions and countenance are letting people know... even more than you think.

Philippians 4:8 (NIV)
Finally, brothers and sisters, whatever is true, whatever is noble, whatever is right, whatever is pure, whatever is lovely, whatever is admirable--if anything is excellent or praiseworthy—THINK about such things.

KINDNESS IN THE MIDDLE

If you count from 1 to 9 you find that the number 5 is in the exact middle... four numbers before it and four numbers after it. There are 9 fruit of the Spirit mentioned in Galatians chapter 5. The fifth fruit, right smack-dab in the MIDDLE of all nine, is the fruit of KINDNESS. I wonder how many people really understand the significance of this. A definitive proof that the Holy Spirit is in your life is that KINDNESS is in the MIDDLE of all that you do. You don't have to TELL people that you have the fruit of the Spirit... you can just SHOW it to them... be KIND!

1 Corinthians 13:4 (NIV)
Love is patient, love is kind.

TODAY'S WISDOM NUGGET
When Jesus needed to get a job done he was a man of FEW WORDS. To calm a storm he said "PEACE, BE STILL" (3 words). To raise a little girl from the dead he said "MAID, ARISE!" (2 words). To allow Peter to walk on the water he said "COME" (1 word). So, why do we think we've got to use a lot of words to get a job done for Him?

MY UMBRELLA OF PROTECTION
May 28 | November 25

I peeked out the window one morning, before my daily morning walk, and I saw dark, overcast skies. So, I pulled out my umbrella and brought it along with me, just in case. I hadn't traveled more than a hundred yards when I noticed a patch of blue sky emerging from behind the dark clouds. As the sky began to clear I felt kind of foolish for toting the umbrella. Who needs an umbrella when there's nothing but blue skies above? But, just a couple of minutes later, the blue sky was overshadowed by ominous, dark clouds which brought a sprinkling rain. Glad I had my umbrella with me then! Funny thing, though... just a couple of minutes later the rain ceased and blue skies reappeared, and once again I was walking under blue skies and sunshine while toting an umbrella.

You know, you just can't worry about what other people think about you for toting an umbrella in uncertain weather! I may have looked kind of foolish, but my main goal was to stay dry... and I succeeded!

We live in a world where the "climate" changes quickly. One minute, things are going well and there's nothing but blue skies... the next, our world is in upheaval and the storms of life seem to be endless. This is the reason why I've chosen to take the Lord with me everywhere I go. Psalm 46:1 says, "God is our refuge and strength, an ever-present help in times of trouble." Now, to some I may look foolish and weak for holding on so tightly to the Lord, especially when it seems that all is going well. I'm no fool, though. I know how quickly everything can change. So, I don't really care what people think of me... my goal is to "stay dry" through the storms of life, and, for the most part, I've succeeded. There is great comfort in knowing that the One who calmed the storm with the words "Peace, Be Still!" is with me... no matter what the forecast may be!

Psalm 27:5 (NIV)
For in the day of trouble he will keep me safe in his dwelling; he will hide me in the shelter of his sacred tent and set me high upon a rock.

TODAY'S FOOD FOR THOUGHT
God is attempting to pour His *limitless* blessing into your *limited* container. It's no wonder the Psalmist exclaimed:
"My cup runneth over." Psalm 23:5

BIBLE FEAR
May 29 | November 26

We would all do well to redefine the word FEAR in our lives. To most, the word FEAR simply means "to be afraid of something" that potentially may cause pain, harm or death. So, people have the FEAR of heights, FEAR of the dark, FEAR of sharks, FEAR of death, FEAR of cancer, etc., etc. But the Bible confuses our thinking when we define FEAR in this way, because all through its pages it tells us to FEAR the Lord. (Deut. 6:13, Josh 24:14, 1 Samuel 12:14, 2 Kings 17:28, Psalm 19:9, etc.). No, the Bible word for FEAR does not mean "to be afraid of something that may harm us." Instead, it means "to reverence, to stand in awe, to respect and honor." So, when I say I FEAR the Lord it is a term of worship and reverence, acknowledging His great POWER and AWE. Because I FEAR Him, I bow in humble reverence before Him.

Now, this is the reason we would all do well to redefine FEAR in our lives. When we say we FEAR heights, FEAR death, FEAR cancer, etc., we are actually saying that we stand in awe of them… that we respect them… that we honor them and bow in their presence. FEAR truly is a word of worship. We bow in humility before the things we FEAR. We give them a powerful place in our lives.

If we FEAR God only, then we have the proper perspective in life. We honor and respect Him, and bow before Him, and Him only. That is FEAR in its purest sense according to the scriptures. Godly FEAR understands that everything is in God's powerful hands. It understands that if we will FEAR God only, everything else falls into its proper place. When people have this correct perspective and definition for FEAR they become emboldened and say things like:

"The Lord is my light and my salvation; WHOM SHALL I FEAR" (Ps. 27:1) and "I trust in God and am not afraid…what can a mere human being do to me" (Ps.56:4)

Yes, a person who truly FEARS God need not have any other FEARS.

TODAY'S WISDOM NUGGET
What happens TO you is temporary. What happens IN you is eternal.
"Christ IN YOU, the hope of glory." Colossians 1:27

TRUSTING SOMEONE ELSE'S EYES
May 30 | November 27

One Sunday afternoon I was backing out of a parking place at a local restaurant. I couldn't see if any cars were coming because a huge truck was blocking my vision. My sister was in the back seat of my truck and she had a better vantage point to see if any cars were coming. She said, "You can back out now... nothing is coming." Totally trusting in her word I backed my truck out of my parking place, not being able to see anything that was behind me.

When I had completely pulled out of the parking place and put my truck in Drive I commented to my sister, "Now, that's what you call walking by Faith, not by Sight!" It was a perfect illustration of what walking by faith means. Trusting the words of somebody who has a better vantage point... trusting the words of someone who can see things more clearly than yourself... trusting the words of someone who can see things that you can't see. Sometimes we mistakenly use the term "blind faith" in our walk of faith. But faith is not blind at all. Faith is trusting in a pair of eyes... just not your own.

You can say that you trust God and that you have faith in Him. But, as long as your foot is on the brake when He says "Accelerate" you're still walking by sight. Romans 10:17 tells us that "Faith comes by hearing, and hearing by the word of God." I'd like to add just a couple of words to that familiar verse without doing any damage to it... "Faith comes by HEARING God tell you what He is SEEING." He has the best vantage point of all... He sees things that you can't see... trust in His eyes... have FAITH!

My Prayer for Today:
"Lord, I know you see things that I can't see. You see things coming my way that I'm completely blind to at the moment. I choose to trust your eyes... not my own."

Hebrews 11:1
Now faith is the substance of things hoped for, the evidence of things NOT SEEN.

TODAY'S WISDOM NUGGET
Fools pursue the "Fountain of Youth"... The wise pursue the "Fountain of Life." *"For with You [God] is the fountain of life." Psalm 36:9*

GATHER UP COURAGE
May 31 | November 28

Have you ever heard the story of Joseph of Arimathea? He was a "secret disciple" of Jesus Christ (John 15:43). He didn't want any of his friends and family to know he followed Jesus because he was afraid of what they might think of him. He was a prominent member of the community. He was a rich man and he was well-respected, but he cared too much about what people thought of his "relationship" with Jesus, so he kept it hidden.

All that changed one day, though, when he saw Jesus hanging on the cross... alone, without his disciples, dead, without a proper burial. Mark 15:43 tells us something rather inspiring about Joseph that happened the day of Jesus' death. It says that Joseph "GATHERED UP COURAGE and went before Pilate, and asked for the body of Jesus." COURAGE! That was the element that he was missing in his relationship with Jesus. Courage to stand up and be counted in the number of those who humbly call themselves "followers of Christ." Courage to cast off fear and timidity, to publicly announce his affiliation with the man who died to save him.

I, too, was once a "secret disciple" of Jesus Christ. I cared too much about what other people thought of me. I was concerned that people might think I was a fanatic or cult member. I was afraid to stand up publicly for Him and announce my affiliation with Him. I can't quite put my finger on when it happened, but somewhere along the way I decided to stand up like a man of conviction, without compromise. I became emboldened by the message that I secretly respected and cherished. Belief overcame fear. I understood what Jesus did for me when He died on the cross for me. I knew it was time to make a complete and total surrender of my personal identity and to name myself as "one of His"... a CHRISTIAN. Why did it take me so long to do it? I lacked something. I had to GATHER UP COURAGE.

Philippians 1:20 (NIV)
I eagerly expect and hope that I will in no way be ashamed, but will have sufficient courage so that now as always Christ will be exalted in my body, whether by life or by death.

YOUR SMILE FOR TODAY
If anyone makes the sarcastic remark to you "Who died and made you King" just say "JESUS!" *"To Him who loved us and washed us from our sins in His own blood, and has made us KINGS...." Revelation 1:5-6*

HE LAID HIS LIFE DOWN
June 1 | November 29

I had fun swimming with my elementary kids at church one Wednesday evening. Somewhere along the way the kids thought it would be "great fun" to see if they could dunk me. For the space of 15 minutes (no exaggeration) I had anywhere from 5 to 8 kids wrapped around my neck, pulling on my legs, pulling on my arms, and screaming in my ears as they did their very best to try to dunk my head beneath the water. My 50-year-old body held up well, however, and none of their most valiant efforts were able to pull my 6'3" frame below the water. When they finally realized that their efforts were futile some of them gave up altogether. So, I said, "Okay, I've proven that you can't take me down so now I'm going to LET you dunk me if you want to." They were all too willing to take me up on my offer. I ended all of my resistance, released my leg muscles and succumbed to the full weight of 8 kids weighing down on me. I sank like a stone to the bottom of the pool. The kids thought it was great that they were able to "bring me down" but I know full well that they didn't do it… I ALLOWED IT.

As I reflected on what happened that night I remembered the words of Jesus when He said, "No man can take my life from me. I lay it down willingly" (John 10:18). The Pharisees, the Sadducees, Pilate and the Roman government all thought that they had a part to play in the "termination" of Jesus. But, actually, all their efforts against the son of God were as futile as those 8 elementary kids trying to dunk their teacher. If Jesus had not willingly laid His life down no "man" would have been able to take his life from Him… HE ALLOWED IT! No, the JEWS didn't kill Jesus… get that idea out of your head. It was a part of His plan to redeem mankind. He let men think that they were snuffing out His life, but in actuality, no government or army of man has the power, has the strength or even the weaponry that would be successful in such an endeavor. No! He LAID HIS LIFE DOWN.

John 10:17 (NLT)
No one can take my life from me. I sacrifice it voluntarily.

TODAY'S FOOD FOR THOUGHT

I wonder how many lies I'm believing right now simply because I believe the word of a man more than the word of God.
"Let God be true, but every man a liar." Romans 3:4

THE PRICE FOR EMPTINESS
June 2 | November 30

I participated in a Storage Unit Auction similar to what you see on the television show "Storage Wars." A dozen people gathered around a small, closet-sized unit as the auctioneer opened the door to reveal the contents within. A rule of the auction is that no one can do anything more than visually inspect the contents from outside the unit… no entrance beyond the door and no opening of boxes is allowed. There was very little to see inside the unit: an old bike, some rusty chains and some clothing. But, there was one very interesting item that everyone saw and took note of… a black safe box with a key sticking in it. The content of the safe box was left to our imagination. Could there be cash in the box? Jewels? Valuable papers?

The bidding began and quickly escalated. When the bidding was over, the unit was purchased for $200. That was a steep price for the inexpensive contents. The bidder was hoping (and gambling) on the thought that the box contained something valuable. My curiosity got the better of me and I asked, "What do you think is in the box?" The gentleman who won the bid grabbed the box, turned the key and opened the lid to reveal the contents… NOTHING! His gamble did not pay off. He held a $200 EMPTY safe box in his hands.

Throughout my life I've seen many people "take a gamble" with their lives, similar to the one this man made at the auction. They invest their time, money and energy in a variety of endeavors hoping to "get lucky" and discover some lasting treasure in life, only to find that their investment and efforts were rewarded with EMPTINESS. The writer of Ecclesiastes reminds us that all this world can offer is "Vanity of vanities, all is vanity" (Ecclesiastes 1:2). Yes, the best this world has to offer us is EMPTINESS… and it doesn't matter if someone has purchased, or owns, more emptiness than you. To be completely filled with empty things is meaningless and pointless.

So, today, I encourage you to do what Jesus requested:

"Store your treasures in heaven, where moths and rust cannot destroy, and thieves do not break in and steal." (Matthew 6:20 NLT)

TODAY'S WISDOM NUGGET
Selective Memory Loss: When you forget how much God has forgiven you, and remember all the things done wrong to you by others.

YOU ARE SEALED!

June 3 | December 1

"Sphragizo" is the Greek word for SEALED. Notice its use in these verses:

Ephesians 1:13 "...you were SEALED in Him with the Holy Spirit of promise."

Ephesians 4:30 "Do not grieve the Holy Spirit of God, by whom you were SEALED for the day of redemption."

Sphragizo definition: To seal...

  a. for security: from Satan
  b. since things sealed up are concealed (as the contents of a letter), to hide, keep in silence, keep secret
  c. in order to mark a person or a thing

If you are a Christian you have been SEALED by the Holy Spirit. God has put His SEAL upon you for security purposes. You are marked as one who belongs to Him. When Satan passes by you He sees God's SEAL upon you... he thinks twice before he messes with you... he knows there will be trouble from God if he does not honor the SEAL that is upon you.

You are SEALED just like an envelope... your contents are protected and hidden from view... there are secret things inside of you that only God Himself knows about and will reveal in His perfect timing.

You are SEALED with God's "stamp of approval." Though you, yourself, did nothing to merit His full approval, yet, because of what Christ did on your behalf, you are fully pleasing to Him. Thus, He puts His mark upon you that you are His child. In essence, His seal upon you, says, "This one is mine."

Isaiah 43:1
Fear not: for I have redeemed thee, I have called thee by thy name; thou art mine.

TODAY'S FOOD FOR THOUGHT

Any good athlete knows that you don't just train in ideal situations. Training should take place in cool temps and hot, in rain and snow, in high altitudes and low. When game day or race day comes you're then prepared for anything that might come your way. I hope your day is filled with comfort and ease... but if not, train well my friend.

A REFUGE AND A FORTRESS
June 4 | December 2

Psalm 91:2
I will say of the Lord, "He is my REFUGE and my FORTRESS..."

God is our protection... just like a FORTRESS or a REFUGE. Do you know the difference between the two? A FORTRESS is a place of protection surrounded by walls. The person inside is safe from enemies or danger on the outside because it is kept completely away by means of the WALLS. But, a REFUGE is slightly different. There might not be any walls around a REFUGE to protect those inside. They are protected nonetheless, simply by a LAW that says, "Anyone who harms those within the boundaries of this REFUGE will be severely punished." In simplified terms, those inside a FORTRESS are protected by WALLS... those inside a REFUGE are protected by LAWS.

There are times in life when we feel "completely surrounded" by God's love and protection. There is a very real sense that HE is surrounding us, just like the walls of a mighty fortress. There are times, however, when the only sense of security and protection that we experience is just in this one thought, "God is my REFUGE... I am IN HIM; therefore I am protected. He has given command that any who would try to bring me harm will do so to their own hurt." Even the most daring demon of Hell will think twice before trespassing upon property that God has said is OFF LIMITS.

If you are a child of God, you are protected... by a WALL and by a LAW. When you understand this, it brings an element of FEARLESSNESS, COURAGE and CONFIDENCE to your life. It will make you say things like, "The Lord is my light and my salvation, whom shall I fear" (Psalm 27:1) and, "If God is for me who can be against me" (Romans 8:31).

My Confession for Today:
"GOD IS MY REFUGE. He has posted a NO TRESPASSING sign on my life. Those who have intentions of bringing me harm will discover that they do so to their own hurt."

TODAY'S WISDOM NUGGET
Don't be concerned that serving others might make you appear to be a "doormat." Remember, Jesus said "I am the door."

FORGIVE AND FORGET

June 5 | December 3

We need to pay closer attention to the words "within" the words that we use. Take, for instance, the word FORGIVE. Notice that it contains the word GIVE. When we FORGIVE, we are GIVING something to somebody... we're giving mercy, the benefit of the doubt, and a second chance. It's a wonderful thing we do when we FORGIVE because we're being GIVING people.

Now, I don't know about you, but as much as I enjoy GIVING, I get an equal amount of pleasure out of GETTING. Everybody likes to GET. That's why we have the word FORGET. When we FORGIVE we GIVE something away, but when we FORGIVE AND FORGET, we GIVE and we also GET. When we FORGET we GET an inward healing... we GET our emotions cleansed... we GET a restored peace because we're no longer dwelling on our past pain... we GET the opportunity to be like God, who not only FORGIVES but also FORGETS our sins and shortcomings.

I know it's not easy... it's hard to FORGET the wrongs done to us... but if we want to GET and not just GIVE we'll have to learn how to FORGET.

Hebrews 8:12
For I will forgive their wickedness and will remember their sins no more."

Psalm 103:12
as far as the east is from the west, so far has he removed our transgressions from us.

TODAY'S FOOD FOR THOUGHT

The most powerful thing you will ever say is "I Forgive You." The second most powerful... "I'll Never Forgive You." After Jesus' resurrection, right after he breathed on his disciples and said, "Receive the Holy Spirit" he then said, "If you forgive anyone his sins, they are forgiven; if you withhold forgiveness from anyone, it is withheld" (John 20:23). Isn't that amazing! He breathed the Holy Spirit on His disciples to awaken their dead spirits, then immediately talked about FORGIVE-NESS. If you have the Holy Spirit inside of you, you have the power to FORGIVE! No, you can't do it on your own... you've got to have the Holy Spirit to assist you... that's why Jesus did it the way He did it!
My Confession for Today: "I will FORGIVE...quickly, often, always."

PLEASE...TRY THIS AT HOME!
June 6 | December 4

SCIENTIFIC EXPERIMENT:
In a well-lit room, stare at a single object for several minutes. Then close your eyes for several seconds. Something interesting happens...the image you just stared at for a prolonged period of time will appear as a negative image upon the darkness of your closed eyelids. The reason? When you stare at something for a prolonged period of time the image gets "burned" into your retina. So, even when you're no longer looking at the object it can still be seen, even when your eyes are closed.

SPIRITUAL EXPERIMENT:
In a very dark world, focus on the things that are good, bright and happy. Do it for minutes and hours at a time. Then, when you close your eyes at night, you will see and experience the good things you focused on throughout the day. That's because a continual focus on all that's good and right gets "burned" into your soul and spirit, and can still be seen even when your eyes are closed.

(NOTE: Completely opposite results can be achieved simply by focusing on all that is bad, evil and negative in our world. But who wants to go to bed at night and see images of evil and negative things all night long... that's just crazy... isn't it?)

My Confession for Today:
I will focus on the good that is around me. I choose to look at the things that are positive in life. I know that negative exists, but it will not steal my focus from the good and positive things that God has placed in my life!

Philippians 4:8
"Finally, brethren, whatever things are true, whatever things are noble, whatever things are just, whatever things are pure, whatever things are lovely, whatever things are of good report, if there is any virtue and if there is anything praiseworthy--meditate on these things."

TODAY'S FOOD FOR THOUGHT
The king of Moab hired Balaam to put a curse on the children of Israel (Numbers 22:6). But, when Balaam was about to pronounce the curse, a blessing came out of his mouth instead. Be reminded today that if you're one whom God has blessed, you cannot be cursed!

WORDS AND THE SOUL
June 7 | December 5

Some people think that we humans are nothing more than bones, muscles, organs, tissue and chemicals all wrapped up in an outer shell of flesh. They don't understand, appreciate or even believe that human beings have a soul and spirit. To them, anything and everything about us can be explained scientifically.

If this is the case, I wonder how these people can explain why it is that unkind words spoken to us can be so painful and damaging? After all, there are no physical wounds that appear when harmful words are spoken… no blood is shed… no bruises appear… no vital organs are pierced or penetrated. Yet, words coming from another person's mouth can be so painful and hurtful that they can make a person stop eating, stop smiling, stop hoping and stop believing. How can invisible breaths of air containing sound waves cause so much damage to a human being? It can't be explained scientifically, because it is a matter of the soul and spirit… science can't explain the realm of the soul or spirit.

Words can hurt us because they can penetrate and wound our souls… that inner part of us that so many of us overlook because we've invested all of our time, money and energy into our flesh (our physical being). The human soul can be helped or hurt by words. The human soul can be encouraged or discouraged by words. Words can get "inside" us… not just in our ears and in our brains, but in our souls and spirits.

If you've been wounded by the words of a fellow human being you are most likely experiencing pain in your soul. You can't go to the Emergency Room and have the wound mended. There is no physical wound to show to the doctor, but there is a wound, nonetheless. So, where do we go when our souls are wounded? Psalm 23 gives the answer as it tells us about our Good Shepherd who leads us beside still waters and RESTORES OUR SOUL. Words from other humans can wound our souls, but a word from God can heal us!

Psalm 107:20 says "He sent His word and healed them."

TODAY'S FOOD FOR THOUGHT
A good word can heal your bones! *"Pleasant words are a honeycomb, Sweet to the soul and healing to the bones." Proverbs 16:24*

IT STARTS WITH A THOUGHT
June 8 | December 6

As I laid in the bed one morning before getting up, I caught myself singing the 1960's song "You're Sixteen" (You're Sixteen, you're beautiful and you're mine.) After repeating it over and over again inside my head I stopped and asked myself, "Where did that come from!?" At first, I thought the song randomly popped up in my head out of nowhere. But as I began to think back to my first waking moments that morning, I remembered that one of my first thoughts was, "What will I eat for breakfast?" I then remembered that the previous night I had bought a box of Oatmeal... the Peaches and Cream variety. When I thought "Peaches and Cream" the lyrics to "You're Sixteen" popped into my head, since the first line of the song says, "You come on like a dream, Peaches and Cream, Lips like strawberry wine." HaHa! Within a moment the mystery to the song that was repeating inside my head was unraveled!

The simple truth of the matter is that almost everything in our lives starts off as just a "simple thought." Like the recurring lyrics of a song stuck in our heads, the smallest thoughts can trigger other thoughts that get converted into words, emotions, feelings, cares, worries, fears and anger. If you're burdened down with cares, worries or fears today, I would challenge you to think back to where it came from. If you will take the time to reflect on it, most likely you will discover that it came from a thought that you entertained, a thought that you dwelled on for longer than was necessary.

One of the key ingredients to overcoming worries, cares and fears in this life comes from "taking our thoughts captive." 2 Corinthians 10:5 says, "We are taking every thought captive to the obedience of Christ." Just because a thought pops up in your head doesn't mean you have to dwell on it. If it doesn't bring comfort, encouragement, joy, or hope then don't entertain it. Take it CAPTIVE. If you don't take IT captive, it will take YOU captive!

My Confession for Today:
I take my thoughts captive! I refuse to dwell on thoughts that will bring me down or lead me to fear, worry or anxiety!

TODAY'S FOOD FOR THOUGHT
Sometimes it's not what's said that gets you into trouble... it's what's repeated. *"He who goes about as a talebearer reveals secrets, But he who is trustworthy conceals a matter."* Proverbs 11:13

WHO WE ARE... WHO WE'RE SUPPOSED TO BE
June 9 | December 7

I was on vacation at the beach and was building a sand sculpture of an elephant. I thought it was coming along nicely, but a woman came up and told me that the tusks of the elephant were wrong. At first I was offended by her comment, but then I humbly asked, "What should I do to make it better?" She gave me a suggestion and I followed her advice. She was right! The alteration I made to the tusks made all the difference in the world. I thanked the woman for helping me with her advice.

The very next day I received word of someone whose feelings were hurt because of some artistic criticism they had received. I texted this person and told them to welcome the criticism as a means of making them better at their craft, explaining to them the way that the woman's words from the previous day had helped me (even though her words initially offended me). In the field of creativity, you've got to be willing to make adjustments by listening to others who can see things that you're not seeing properly. That's the way you grow and get better at what you do. But, this can't happen unless you're humble enough to receive words of advice, and yes, even criticism.

I say all of this to relay this one thought… being humble enough to admit that you might be wrong is the first step to becoming better. I see people every day who want people to "accept them the way they are" so they reject any words of advice or wisdom that suggest that changes need to be made. If you're so strongly entrenched in who you "presently are" that you fail to accept advice from others, then you can't become the person you are "supposed to be." Yes, you are loved and appreciated for who you "presently are" but you are also on the way to "becoming who you will be." Never forget that. And most often the changes that are needed to get you to where you're supposed to be will come by way of wisdom and advice passed on by others… people who see things about you that you can't see.

2 Corinthians 3:18
But we all… are changed into the same image from glory to glory, even as by the Spirit of the Lord.

TODAY'S FOOD FOR THOUGHT
God has promised that goodness and mercy will FOLLOW ME
if I will FOLLOW HIM. It's important who you follow!

GOD IS GOOD
June 10 | December 8

While I was talking with a lady many years ago, we got into a discussion about the goodness of God. I remember her saying, "When I talk about how good God is something comes over me and I almost can't contain myself!" There have been many occasions in my Christian experience where I have felt this very same way. There is a popular worship chorus by Chris Tomlin called "Good, Good Father" which has an incredible effect on me when I hear it or sing it.

I was thinking about the goodness of God recently, and asked the Lord why the mention of His goodness creates such a powerful effect in people. I believe these are things that He spoke to my heart in reply to my question:

> There is divine energy released when TRUTH is spoken out loud. Jesus himself told of the great power that TRUTH possesses when he said, "The TRUTH will set you free." The greater the TRUTH that is spoken, the greater impact and effect that it has. There is NO GREATER TRUTH that can be spoken than these 3 simple words "GOD IS GOOD." It is the most perfect and pure TRUTH that exists. When you speak it in your life, and over your situations, you are releasing the power of divine TRUTH that "sets free."

My Prayer for Today:
"Lord, thank You for this word of truth! Lord, You see the world I live in that is so enamored with lies and deception. I often ask You 'Why are so many people sad and depressed' and You remind me 'Because they haven't received the truth.' Truth is so rarely proclaimed or heard. Lies have no power to give hope, joy, light or peace, but when I speak Your truth a great power is released, and the greatest truth I can release into this world is this......GOD IS GOOD!"

Psalm 86:5 (NAS)
For You, Lord, are good, and ready to forgive, And abundant in loving kindness to all who call upon You.

TODAY'S WORD OF ENCOURAGEMENT
You weren't born to SUCCUMB... You were born to OVERCOME!
SUCCUMB (verb): To submit to an overpowering force; to give up.
OVERCOME (verb): To defeat in competition or conflict. (Rev. 12:11)

"IF IT IS POSSIBLE"
June 11 | December 9

Matthew 26:39 (NLT)
He [Jesus] went on a little farther and bowed with his face to the ground, praying, "My Father! IF IT IS POSSIBLE, let this cup of suffering be taken away from me. Yet I want your will to be done, not mine."

We often say that nothing is IMPOSSIBLE for God, and rightly so. Luke 1:37 says, "For with God nothing shall be impossible" (The words of the Angel Gabriel to the Virgin Mary). But, in the Garden of Gethsemane, as Jesus travails in prayer on the night of His betrayal, knowing the suffering he is about to face, He prays the words, "Father, IF IT IS POSSIBLE, let this cup of suffering be taken away from me." Jesus knew that He had to suffer for mankind to be redeemed, but His prayer revealed a hope in His heart that there might be some other way. Was there any other way for mankind to be saved? Was there anything else that could be done besides Jesus dying for our sins? Was that really the only solution?

Some in today's society seem to think there are other ways that mankind can get "right" with God besides through Jesus. If that were the case, though, surely God would have honored Jesus' prayer for the cup of suffering to pass from Him. Jesus asked God point-blank, "IF IT IS POSSIBLE let this cup pass from me." You know the rest of the story. Jesus went on to be mocked, tried and crucified within the next 24 hours after that prayer was prayed, showing that there has only ever been ONE IMPOSSIBILITY with God... it was IMPOSSIBLE to redeem mankind any other way than through the death of His Son Jesus.

Thank you Jesus, for being obedient to the Father's plan to redeem mankind the only way that was possible... through Your sacrifice.

Acts 4:12 (NIV)
Salvation is found in NO ONE ELSE, for there is no other name under heaven given to mankind by which we must be saved.

TODAY'S FOOD FOR THOUGHT
DELAYED GRATIFICATION is an economic term that has spiritual connotations. Here's the definition: "The ability to forgo an immediate pleasure or reward in order to gain a more substantial one later." A substantial reward awaits you, child of God!

NOT TO BE SERVED, BUT TO SERVE
June 12 | December 10

I read the story of Paul's shipwreck on the island of Malta to my elementary kids at church. We read about how the crew of the ship went out to gather sticks to build a fire and Paul joined them. As he was gathering sticks a poisonous viper bit him and latched on to his hand, and the island people watched to see if he would die from the bite. As the story goes, Paul shook the serpent off into the fire and continued to gather sticks. The snake's venom had no effect on this powerful man of God.

But, this is not the point that I wanted to make about the story. The thing I pointed out to the young men in the room was that even though Paul was a powerful man of God, he was showing a servant's heart as he collected sticks along with the other men. He didn't think that such a task was "beneath him." I told the kids, "No matter how 'great' you might be (both in this world's eyes or in the kingdom of God) you must always remember the importance of being a servant."

As soon as I said those words, one of the boys who has a keen spiritual perception said, "He didn't come to 'be served but to serve'!" A chill went down my spine. It was probably two years earlier when I taught that memory verse from Matthew 20:28 to this group, and that little boy still had it tucked away in his spirit, and understood the connection to this lesson. Talk about being blessed as a teacher! I was thankful that I had a part to play in that child's development as a Christian... and as a servant for God's kingdom.

Remember, Jesus didn't come to be served, but to serve... Paul didn't come to be served, but to serve... you aren't here to be served, but to serve.

Matthew 20:26-28 (NLT)
"But among you it will be different. Whoever wants to be a leader among you must be your servant, and whoever wants to be first among you must become your slave. For even the Son of Man came not to be served but to serve others and to give his life as a ransom for many."

YOUR SMILE FOR TODAY
Sometimesyoujustneedalittlespace.Timesetapartfromeverythingelse-soyoucanthinkaboutwhereonethingendsandanotherthingbegins.
Howterriblelifewouldbeifyoudidn'thavethespaceyouneeded.

THE "PLACE" YOU'RE SUPPOSED TO BE

June 13 | December 11

Abraham's father, Terah, was traveling with his family to Canaan but stopped short and settled in Haran, where he later died. After Terah's death, God called Abraham to continue the journey that his father had started. Abraham listened to God and moved into Canaan. It was "the PLACE he was supposed to be." He was prosperous and successful in Canaan. He had a son, Isaac, who lived in Canaan all of his life. Isaac, too, was prosperous and successful, continually walking in the favor and blessing of God. Canaan was "the PLACE he was supposed to be." Isaac had a son name Jacob who lived in Canaan most of his life. He was prosperous and successful because he was in "the PLACE he was supposed to be." But, something happened that made Jacob (Israel) and his family move from Canaan to Egypt... an unfortunate circumstance... a famine.

Had God called Jacob to move to Egypt? No. Canaan was "the PLACE he was supposed to be." Yes, Egypt had the things he and his family needed (food and provision), but he was never told to leave the place God had called his grandfather Abraham to.

You know the rest of the story, right? Israel's decedents, who were once blessed and prosperous living in Canaan (the PLACE they were supposed to be) soon became slaves in Egypt (the PLACE they weren't supposed to be). The Israelites endured 400 years of slavery because they left the PLACE of God's blessing and favor. Just imagine that! There were Israelites whose fathers, grandfathers and great-grandfathers never knew anything but slavery, even though they were descendants of some of the richest men on earth... the Patriarchs! But, God raised up Moses to tell Pharaoh, "Let my people GO!" Where were they going to? Back to Canaan Land... The Promised Land... THE PLACE THEY WERE SUPPOSED TO BE!

Here's what we learn from this story. If you will stay in the PLACE God wants you to be you will be blessed and have favor. If you choose to move from the PLACE God wants you to be you will, most likely, endure hardship and difficulty, but God will reach out to you to show you a way to get back to "the PLACE you're supposed to be."

1 Chronicles 17:9
Also I will ordain a PLACE for my people Israel, and will plant them, and they shall dwell in their place, and shall be moved no more....

SHAKE IT OFF!

June 14 | December 12

One Sunday morning I was sitting on the front row at church, waiting for the service to start, when I looked down on the floor and saw several scattered piles of dirt and grass clippings. Someone had unwittingly tracked the debris into the church with their shoes. I asked a couple of people standing nearby to check their shoes for dirt, and everyone's shoes were clean. So, I checked my own shoes and discovered that I was the culprit who had tracked dirt into "the house of the Lord." I walked delicately to the door so as not to track more dirt, and when I got outside I stomped my feet trying to shake off the remaining debris from my shoes.

The next morning, while on my morning walk, I saw dirt and debris once again building up on the edges of my shoes and I remembered what Jesus told his disciples, "Shake the dust off of your feet" (Matthew 10:14). I got a new understanding about that scripture. You see, we go to places in life that sometimes leave a "residue" on us that has to be shaken off. When we're surrounded by anger and arguments, when we're confronted with bitterness, when we're around unforgiving and jealous people, those things tend to "contaminate" our souls and pollute our spirits. If we're not careful we will carry those things around with us and actually become unwitting culprits in spreading the negativity, simply because we were standing in it or nearby it.

When I noticed the dirt and debris on my shoes that Monday morning after my morning walk, before I entered my house, I shook the dust off my feet. I didn't want to scatter dirt and debris in my home. My home is my sanctuary. My home is my refuge from the world. I want it to be clean and uncontaminated. We've got to "shake it off" if we want to live clean lives, free from all the pollution and negativity around us. It's that simple.

2 Corinthians 7:1
Having therefore these promises, dearly beloved, let us cleanse ourselves from all filthiness of the flesh and spirit.

TODAY'S WORD OF ENCOURAGEMENT

If you hear a voice inside you that says, "What's the use" or, "This situation is hopeless" you can guarantee you're hearing the voice of your enemy, the devil. When you're facing an obstacle GOD WILL NEVER encourage you to quit or give up hope… NEVER.

JUDGE NOT
June 15 | December 13

On my way to church one night I was driving behind a truck that appeared to be tailgating the truck ahead of it. I followed along behind the two trucks in the left lane for over a mile as we drove along at about 55 miles per hour. The "tailgating" truck stayed the same tight distance from the truck ahead of it (less than 15 feet away) for the whole mile. I was concerned and, to be honest, a bit angry about the situation. I imagined how I would have felt if someone was tailgating me that closely for so long.

Both trucks slowed down to take a left turn and I followed behind them. It was then, as they were turning, that I realized the front truck was actually towing the truck behind it with a 15 foot chain. I laughed when I realized that my anger at the "tailgater" was completely unfounded!

Once again I was reminded that we don't always perceive things the way they really are, so we shouldn't be so hasty to pass judgment against others. When I think about how "worked up" I got about something that wasn't even happening… that shows you just how deceptive our own perceptions can be!

My Confession for Today:
I will be quick to extend mercy and to believe the best about the people and situations that I face today.

Luke 6:37 (NIV)
Do not judge, and you will not be judged. Do not condemn, and you will not be condemned. Forgive, and you will be forgiven.

TODAY'S WORD OF ENCOURAGEMENT
Very few artists like to have people peering over their shoulder while they're at work. They only want you to see the completed project.
Not so with God. He does His artistry in You while everyone is watching. Too often people critique His Work as if they're looking at the finished piece. But the Master is not afraid to let others see His Masterpiece in the making.
"And I am sure that God, who began the good work within you, will continue his work until it is finally finished on that day when Christ Jesus comes back again."
Philippians 1:6 NLT

THE END
June 16 | December 14

When Jesus heard that his friend Lazarus was sick he delayed going to him, and said to his disciples, "This sickness will not end in death…." If you know the story, however, you remember that Lazarus did actually die from his sickness and Jesus had to go and raise him from the dead. (John 11)

So, it almost seems contradictory, doesn't it?! Did Jesus lie? Did Jesus get his "wires crossed" with God? Did he misinterpret what God had spoken to his spirit?

Let's go back and look at exactly what Jesus said. He said, "This sickness will not END in death" (emphasis on the word END). As the old saying goes "It isn't over until it's over." In the story of Lazarus, Lazarus DID die, but that's not where the story ENDED. He was raised from the dead by the loving, caring, powerful Messiah. So, you see, Jesus was completely correct... Lazarus' sickness didn't end in death. It ENDED in a resurrection!

Do you know WHERE you are in the story of your life that God is writing? There are twists and turns in every good story that's ever been written, but the story isn't over until you see the words "THE END." The story of your life has probably been filled with drama, twists and turns, and seeming dead-ends, but don't panic. You're only in the middle of the story. Don't let the devil lie to you and tell you that it's THE END. It's not over until God says it's over!

My Confession for Today:
"I know that God has good plans for my life. Everything is working together for my good because I'm called according to His purpose. When things aren't going good at the moment I will not get disheartened... I know my story will not END with bad news.

Jeremiah 29:11
For I know the thoughts that I think toward you, saith the LORD, thoughts of peace, and not of evil, to give you an EXPECTED END.

TODAY'S WISDOM NUGGET
Your Attention is one of the most valuable things you possess. That's why we have the phrase "PAY attention." If you don't PAY attention it will COST you. *"PAY ATTENTION and turn your ear to the sayings of the wise; apply your heart to what I teach." Proverbs 22:17*

CONNECTED TO AN ADAM
June 17 | December 15

I had a sobering word to deliver to my friends at the Men's Home Bible Study one night. I asked the men, "How many of you have children?" Three men raised their hands. I asked, "Have you realized yet that your kids are connected to you, both in regards to your failures AND your successes?" When you have a failure, the truth is that it doesn't just affect you… it also affects those that you are connected to. The same holds true for successes. When we are blessed and victorious, it affects those we are connected to.

This is a very important, underlying theme in the Bible. Open up the first pages of the Bible in Genesis and you discover that our great-grandfather Adam had a tremendous failure, and his failure didn't just affect him… it affected his children, his grandchildren and all that followed in his footsteps. His failure was "passed down" to future generations. You and I are the "seed of Adam." His DNA was passed down to us because we are connected to him.

But there's good news! Jesus came to Earth as "The Second Adam."

So also it is written, "The first man, Adam, became a living soul." The last Adam became a life-giving spirit. - 1 Corinthians 15:45.

Those who choose to identify with Him, who CONNECT with Him by getting BORN AGAIN, get connected to His success and victory over death, Hell and the grave.

We are CONNECTED to one or the other… The First Adam or The Last Adam. If we never connect with the Last Adam through rebirth then we are ultimately connected to The First Adam and his failure. But, if we choose Jesus as our Lord, we get connected to The Last Adam and His success and victory. Do you know which Adam you are connected to?

1 Corinthians 15:47 (NIV)
The first man was of the dust of the earth; the second man is of heaven.

TODAY'S WORD OF EXHORTATION
RESILIENT (adjective) - 1. Able to spring back into shape after bending, stretching, or being compressed. 2. Able to withstand or recover quickly from difficult conditions. This is my confession for today: *"I am RESILIENT… I recover quickly from difficult conditions."*

IRRATIONAL FEAR
June 18 | December 16

One morning, on my daily morning walk, I passed by a wooded area and was startled by the sound of an angry man's gruff voice. "Stop right there", the stern voice shouted. I couldn't see anyone nor could I tell from which direction the voice was coming. I wasn't sure if the man was yelling at me or not, so I stopped in my tracks. I heard the voice again, in an even angrier tone say, "Get over here, right now!" Was he talking to me? Could he have a gun? Was he wanting to rob me? I was having all types of fear-filled scenarios run through my head as I stood there. Then, I heard the sound of a dog barking in the woods. The man called out again, "Get over here!" Phew! I realized he wasn't yelling at me but at his dog who had run away from him. One last time he yelled "Get over here, Fluff-Fluff!" His dog's name was "Fluff-Fluff!" I couldn't help but laugh out loud when I heard him call the dog's name. There's no way I should be afraid of a man who would call his dog "Fluff-Fluff." I started back on my walk, amused by the fear that had stopped me in my tracks just moments earlier.

Isn't it funny how powerful the emotion of FEAR can be? To be honest, I was just a little bit disappointed at my first reactions to this situation. After all, I claim to have a relationship with a Mighty, Powerful God. I've often quoted the scripture "Greater is He that is in me than He that is in the world" and "if God is for me who can be against me." But, just for a moment I forgot all of that and caved in to an irrational FEAR. I'm so glad that man named his dog Fluff-Fluff, though! When I heard that name ringing out through the woods my fear dissipated and laughter took its place.

One day in the not-too-distant future, I know that every fear I've ever faced on this planet will dissolve and will seem like pure nonsense when I stand before Almighty God, and fully realize all of the greatness that He possesses that I never fully comprehended here on Earth. Yes, when I get to Heaven I have a feeling I will spend a good bit of time laughing at how absurd all of my earthly fears and worries were.

Isaiah 41:10 (ESV)
Fear not, for I am with you; be not dismayed, for I am your God

TODAY'S FOOD FOR THOUGHT
Even the devil is not an atheist! *"Thou believest that there is one God; thou doest well: the devils also believe, and tremble." James 2:19*

DON'T MOVE WITHOUT HIM
June 19 | December 17

Years ago, on my daily morning walks I was trying to train my dog, Lily, (a German Schnauzer) not to cross the street when cars were coming. One day I thought I'd try something new. As we were walking along we got to the place where we cross a very busy street. I stopped at the curb and waited and Lily waited with me. No cars were coming, but instead of going ahead and crossing, I waited... and Lily waited with me, looking up at me from time-to-time as if to say, "Can we cross now?" I waited a full minute without a single car passing by. We could have crossed at any time but I wanted Lily to know that she shouldn't cross until I crossed... until "I" was sure that it was safe. She passed the test.

I mused at what might have been going on inside her head as we stood there waiting for no particular reason. Perhaps she thought, "Doesn't my master realize there aren't any cars coming?" Or, maybe, "Why are we waiting here so long anyway?" Maybe even, "Does he know something I don't know?" Most likely, however, there was probably NOTHING going on inside her head at all. As I laughed inside myself at the thought, a more important thought came to me. Is it possible that those times in our lives where seemingly nothing is happening, where it seems like we're waiting at one of life's intersections for no apparent reason, that God is actually training us? That He is teaching us not to make a move WITH-OUT HIM... preparing us for future moments where hearing His directions will be vital to our very survival? Yes, my friend, it's quite possible that you are "in training" at this very moment without even knowing it.

Exodus 33:14-15 (NAS)
And He said, "My presence shall go with you, and I will give you rest."
Then he [Moses] said to Him, "If Your presence does not go with us, do not lead us up from here.

TODAY'S WISDOM NUGGET
There are three "sisters" you need by your side in life:
1. reSISTER - *"RESIST the devil and he will flee." James 4:7.*
2. asSISTER - *"She's quick to ASSIST anyone in need, reaches out to help the poor." Proverbs 31:20.*
3. perSISTER - *"I was happy when some friends arrived and brought the news that you PERSIST in following the way of Truth." 3 John 1:3.*

CONFIDE
June 20 | December 18

One night, after I had conducted a Bible Study, an acquaintance of mine asked to speak to me privately. Though we had talked before in a group setting, this was the first time we had talked "one-on-one." He shared with me a problem he was going through and wanted my input. I was honored that he thought highly enough of me that he would confide in me, and that got me thinking. "Confide" is the root word of "Confidence" so, obviously, when you confide in someone you're showing confidence in them and in their ability either to help out or to give good advice. When I realized how good it made me feel for this young man to ask my advice, I believe I got a small glimpse of what God experiences when we come to Him in prayer, putting confidence in His ability to help us out.

Some may think, "Surely God must tire of hearing our problems and our needs," but I have a suspicion that the opposite is true. I think He is honored that we think highly enough of Him that we would seek out His advice and His counsel in the situations of our lives... that He is not just another one of the many "faces in the crowd" but, rather, One with Whom we seek a moment alone that we might CONFIDE in Him. Yes, I believe He is honored.

Isaiah 26:4 (Darby Bible Translation)
Confide ye in Jehovah for ever; for in Jah, Jehovah, is the rock of ages.

FULL... OF EMPTINESS!

Take 100 empty cereal boxes and fill up your cupboards with them. You might then say, "My cupboards are full" but is that an accurate statement? Sometimes the feeling of emptiness that we humans experience does not come from literal emptiness but rather from being full... of empty things. Eph. 3:19 says, "And to know this love that surpasses knowledge-that you may be filled to the measure of all the fullness of God." The fullness of God... now that's FULL.

TODAY'S WISDOM NUGGET
Don't take to heart every word of criticism against you... nor every word of praise. *"The crucible for silver and the furnace for gold, but man is tested by the praise he receives." Proverbs 27:21*

I'M BEING SHAPED
June 21 | December 19

Have you ever heard the saying "we are shaped by our experiences?" The inference is that "who we are" is a result of "what happens to us" in our lives. Although there is truth in that saying, I prefer to look at it a different way. I don't think it is just coincidence that Jeremiah refers to God as a POTTER. Jeremiah 18:6 says, "Behold, as the clay is in the potter's hand, so are ye in mine hand." God is the One who is shaping us. I am not shaped by my past, by my hurt, by my pain, or by my circumstances. No, I am being shaped by God. He has me on His potter's wheel. It is the pressure from His Hands that forms me. If you look close enough you will see His fingerprints on me - the fingerprints are still fresh because the job is not completed. Hardened clay cannot be molded. It must stay soft and pliable for the Potter to work with it.

"Lord God, keep me soft and pliable so You can shape me into the vessel You desire me to be. Do not let me get hard and brittle because of past hurts and experiences. Keep me on Your wheel. Spin me, turn me around, apply Your pressure.... SHAPE ME!"

Isaiah 64:8
But now, O LORD, thou art our father; we are the clay, and thou our potter; and we all are the work of thy hand.

"WHO" IS IN YOU IS GREATER THAN "WHAT" IS IN YOU

You've probably heard this scripture verse before, "Greater is He that is in you than he that is in the world" (1 John 4:4). Well, I'd like to add a thought to this verse that in no way detracts from its truth: "Greater is He that is in you than anything else that is IN YOU." That includes everything from the common cold, to confusion, to cancer cells... you name it. If it's "in you" (your body or soul), it is less than the Greater One who is "in you". So if you're struggling with emotional issues or sickness today be encouraged by this thought... the Greater One is in you! Be blessed!

TODAY'S FOOD FOR THOUGHT
If you "know better" but won't "do better" things won't "get better."
"Be ye doers of the word, and not hearers only." James 1:22

CAN YOU TAKE A PUNCH?
June 22 | December 20

Occasionally, I enjoy watching MMA cage fights on TV. I have often wondered what it would feel like to get punched in the face by one of those guys. Could I take the punch? Would I fall to the floor? Would I cry like a baby? Well, one night I inadvertently got my answer!

I went to the garage to get something out of my truck and didn't turn on the lights to see what I was doing. I opened the door directly into my left cheek bone with full force. I heard a giant thud inside my head and everything went pitch black for just a moment. I grimaced in pain as I held on to my throbbing cheek bone. I guess it was about 30 seconds there where I did nothing except hold my face in my hands, trying to recover from the massive "blow."

After nursing my cheekbone with an icepack and having a good night's sleep I awoke the next morning to find no damage done except for a small knot under my left eye (and a humbled ego). That morning as I thought again about the previous night's "moment of stupidity" I also thought about those MMA guys as they fight in the octagon. They get hit directly in the face continuously and just keep right on fighting. They don't pull off into the corner and nurse their throbbing cheekbone each time they get hit. There's no time for it. They take the punch and then return with one of their own. After receiving my "truck-door-punch" I had a greater respect for them.

So, here's a question for you: CAN YOU TAKE A PUNCH? When life hits you hard can you take the punch and keep on fighting? Do you have to have a support group every time something bad happens to you? When things are going rough, do you try to draw up some kind of truce with the devil, "If you don't hit me I won't hit you." When you're pinned to the floor and feel like you can't get up do you just "tap out"? Listen to these words that the apostle Paul said when he was going through all of his trials and struggles: "We are hard pressed on every side, but not crushed; perplexed, but not in despair; persecuted, but not abandoned; struck down, but not destroyed" (2 Corinthians 4:8-9). I like the way that I heard one preacher say it: "I'm knocked down, but not knocked out!"

Ephesians 6:12 (NLT)
For we are not fighting against flesh-and-blood enemies, but against evil rulers and authorities of the unseen world.

3 MEASURES OF MEAL
June 23 | December 21

"The kingdom of Heaven is like unto leaven which a woman took and hid in 3 measures of meal till the whole was leavened."
(Matthew 13:33 - King James Version).

I was studying this parable of Jesus one night and discovered that the New International Version (NIV) doesn't say, "3 Measures of Meal" but rather, says, "Sixty Pounds of flour." This is one reason why I don't always like newer translations. You see, I saw something in that scripture as I read it for the hundredth time that I never noticed before... it was the number "3" in the King James Version. I suppose I thought the number 3 was just an informational fact found in the parable in all my past readings of the verse. But that night it hit me. The "3" is important! Why, look at the verse number that it's found in, for Heaven's Sakes! Matthew 13:33... there are 3 "threes" found just in the verse numbering. Then you find the number 3 within the verse itself. The number 3 means something in this verse, and the New International Version translators missed it, and removed this number that has meaning so they could better describe the full amount of flour in modern terms (60 pounds of flour).

So, why should the NIV not have substituted "3 measures of meal" with "60 pounds of flour"? Because the 3 represents a human being's triune nature... Spirit, Soul and Body. The kingdom of Heaven, as this parable shows, is hidden within the triune nature of man. It is unseen (hidden) inside the spirit of a man and slowly works its way into the soul and the body until the human is completely and entirely affected by the work of God's Kingdom in every area of his life. Yes, it is unseen and hidden for a while, but as the spirit within a man takes hold of God's Kingdom the "yeast" rises and permeates within, and eventually a man's life is infiltrated by the Kingdom power that brings change in every area of life.

Friend, you are not "60 pounds of flour." You are "3 measures of meal." You are Spirit, Soul and Body! May the kingdom of Heaven work in you today... changing you from the inside out!

TODAY'S WORD OF EXHORTATION
If you DWELL IN the secret place don't DWELL ON your problems.
"He that dwells in the secret place of the Most High shall abide under the shadow of the Almighty." Psalm 91:1

OLD... BUT NOT COLD

June 24 | December 22

I was quietly worshiping the Lord one Sunday morning in church when an old gentleman sat down just two seats from me. I had never seen the elderly man before. He appeared to be in his late 80s, quite possibly even early 90s. He was smartly dressed in a stylish brown suit and yellow tie. He was very distinguished looking.

Moments later, I glanced in his direction and caught a glimpse of him with eyes closed and hands raised in worship as a contemporary worship song was being played. It was obvious to me that he was not so engaged in worship because of the style of the music being played, or because of the song selection, but simply because he loved the "One" that was being sung to. I don't mind telling you that I was moved to tears to see such an expression of worship from an older person... so removed from me in years, yet so close to me in heart.

I have now seen the man I hope to be as time progresses for me. Times change, seasons of life change, people in our lives change, physical appearance changes, styles and tastes change, but one thing remains the same through our years.... God does not change. He will forever be worshiped.

We will never outgrow worship, and never reach a place where it is no longer necessary. As a matter of fact, if we're planning on going to Heaven we should be preparing ourselves for an eternity of worship. Thank you Lord for sending that old man to me that Sunday morning and letting me see the face of my future... a future where "growing old" doesn't mean "growing cold."

Psalm 92:12-14 (NAS)
The righteous man will flourish like the palm tree, He will grow like a cedar in Lebanon. Planted in the house of the LORD, They will flourish in the courts of our God. They will still yield fruit in old age.

TODAY'S WISDOM NUGGET
3 reasons why you may not be seeing things correctly:
1) Wrong perspective - You're looking at things from the wrong angle.
2) Wrong focus - You're seeing clearly but you're not looking at the right thing. 3) Wrong magnification - Small things can look gigantic when you're looking at them under a magnifying glass.

FOR HIS NAME'S SAKE

June 25 | December 23

I was teaching a group of elementary kids a Bible Lesson from Psalm 23. We got to the place where it says, "He leads me in the paths of righteousness for His name's sake." One little boy said, "What does that mean, 'for His name's sake?'" I asked the little boy what his father's last name was and he told me. Then I asked, "And what is your last name?" He replied, "Same as his." I said, "So, you carry your father's name around wherever you go. The things you do as you go down the pathway of life, both good and bad, will have a reflection on your father because you carry his name. You don't want to do anything to hurt your father's name do you?" The little boy very emphatically replied, "No!"

Likewise, those who are children of God carry His name wherever they go. God won't lead you down the wrong path… it's not good for His name. Follow the path He has for you and it will always be good for you… and it will bring honor to His name.

Psalm 23:3 (English Standard Version)
He restores my soul; He leads me in the paths of righteousness For His name's sake.

IN COURAGE

The root word of ENCOURAGE is "courage." When you encourage someone you are attempting to put COURAGE IN that person. Courage is the main inward ingredient needed when fighting a battle against an intimidating enemy. Without it, warriors become wimps. So, you see, encouragement is not given so that people can ball up on the couch with a cup of hot cocoa and feel a warm fuzzy… it's given to stir up the heart of the warrior within us so we can stand up and fight our enemy. Be encouraged!

1 Corinthians 16:13 (NIV)
Be on your guard; stand firm in the faith; be men of courage; be strong.

TODAY'S WORD OF EXHORTATION

There are only two things that keep us from learning something new:
1. Fear (which says "I can't")
2. Stubbornness (which says "I won't").
"I CAN do all things through Christ who gives me strength." Phil. 4:13

YOU TOOK THE BLAME
June 26 | December 24

When I was 5 years old, my mother called me and my brother and sisters in from playing in the front yard. She sat us down on the couch and said, "I want to know which one of you scratched this coffee table!" Sure enough, there on the front edge of the coffee table were several deep scratches etched into the finish. Nobody confessed. So, she announced, "Nobody will be leaving that couch until someone confesses." We sat there for several minutes and no one admitted to the crime. My mother left the room. The sound of our neighborhood friends laughing and playing in our front yard beckoned us to come up with an answer to our dilemma… and fast. Since I was the youngest of the bunch my brother and sisters determined that I should be the scapegoat. So they convinced me that I did the deed and even concocted a story for me to tell my mom of how I did it. I then went to my mother in the kitchen and confessed to scratching of the table. I received my punishment as my brother and sisters went out to play and I stayed inside, grounded for the day. At Thanksgiving and Christmastime we often retell that story and laugh about it. To this day, I still proclaim my innocence even though I'm the one who received the blame and the punishment.

2000 years ago a similar scene took place, but with much greater consequences. Sin was running rampant in the world and justice called for the punishment of all wrong-doers. Table-scratching was not on the list of crimes on this day. No, instead it was things like lying, cheating, stealing, killing, hatred, sexual immorality, bigotry, etc., etc. All of mankind was guilty, yet there was ONE who was completely innocent that took the blame and received the punishment. Yes, I speak of Jesus Christ and His substitutionary death. No one was going anywhere except directly to hell until someone took the blame for the wrong. Jesus stepped up and took the blame, and the punishment we deserved.

Just for a moment today, think about the great thing that was done for you 2000 years ago when an innocent man took your punishment, and be reminded of how deserving He is of a special word of thanks from a grateful heart. "Lord Jesus, Praise Your Name… You Took the Blame!"

Isaiah 53:5
But he was wounded for OUR transgressions, he was bruised for OUR iniquities.

THE EXHORTER
June 27 | December 25

"What is an exhorter?" That was the question I was asked at the Men's Bible Study after I said, "Tonight I'm going to be an exhorter and not just an encourager." So, I proceeded to use a little illustration to explain the difference between an encourager and exhorter, and it went something like this:

> You are watching a marathon. Runners are passing by you on their long trek of 26 miles. You notice one runner stumble and fall to the ground. He holds his knee in painful agony as blood begins to trickle from a wound resulting from the fall. You see a person run out to him. It is an encourager. He cleans up the wound on the runner's knee, puts his arm around his shoulder and comforts him with the words, "It's okay, everything is okay. This happens to all of us at one time or another in life, but you're going to be alright. As a matter of fact this very same thing happened to me and I'm still alive today. It's not the end of the world."
>
> Then you see another person run out to him. It is an exhorter. He pulls the runner off of the ground to his feet, points him toward the finish line as he pushes the runner in that direction and yells "RUN! You can still win this race. It's not over yet… GET GOING!

Both the encourager and the exhorter care about the runner. The difference is this: The encourager cares about where the runner IS, and the exhorter cares about where the runner IS GOING. We will meet both of these people throughout our lives and we desperately need them both.

Today, you're in a race, whether you realize it or not. You may have stumbled and fallen along the way, but the race isn't over. We've all fallen at one time or another. So, get back up on your feet and RUN! There's a finish line to cross and you'll never get there sitting on the ground nursing your wounds. That's your "exhortation" for today!

1 Corinthians 9:24
Do you not know that those who run in a race all run, but only one receives the prize? Run in such a way that you may win.

184

GET OVER IT!
June 28 | December 26

GET OVER IT! I've heard people say that phrase and it sounds like a very uncaring way of telling somebody that their problem isn't that big of a deal. Well, I'd like to add a new twist to this old familiar phrase. If you're dealing with a major problem, you need to see it from a different perspective. If you're UNDER the problem looking up at it, it will look enormous to you because you have the wrong perspective. If you're BESIDE the problem looking at it, it will still look like a very formidable foe. But if you'll GET OVER IT and look down on it from a higher elevation, you will see the problem from God's view point and it really won't seem as enormous as you imagined it to be. Ephesians 2:6 tells us that we are "seated with Christ in Heavenly places." Heavenly places... that's the perspective we should have when we view our problems. The right perspective changes everything. So if you're dealing with what seems to be like an insurmountable problem, I say this with utmost compassion and sincerity... "GET OVER IT!"

Romans 16:20 (NAS)
The God of peace will soon crush Satan UNDER your feet.

DON'T "DIS" ME

The Romans had an interesting name for the "god of the underworld". It was DIS PATER. As the years went by the name was shortened to DIS. DIS was the equivalent to the Greek god HADES and to THE DEVIL of the Bible. So, almost every word that starts with the 3 letters "D-I-S" can be directly related to the DEVIL... seriously!

If you're DIScouraged you might say that you're DEVILcouraged. If you have a DISease it wouldn't be wrong to call it a DEVILease. Feeling DISsatisfied? You guessed it... you're really DEVILsatisfied. Children who DISobey their parents are DEVILobeying. You get the picture, right? So, if you're feeling a little DIScontented in your life and want to break free from all of life's DIStractions, I'd like to suggest that you pray and read God's Word to end the DISorder you've been experiencing. I don't think you'll be DISappointed!

2 Corinthians 2:11 (NAS)
So that no advantage would be taken of us by Satan, for we are not ignorant of his schemes.

THE HEART AND HEAD CONNECTION
June 29 | December 27

When blood stops flowing from the heart to the brain the result is classified as "clinical death." I'll say it this way: "A person is dead when there is no longer activity between the heart and the brain." Isn't that interesting! Our brain is so totally dependent upon our heart that a glitch in the connection between the two can cause death. If we take this knowledge into our soul/spirit realm it can give us greater understanding about how we are wired by God.

We live in a world where so much emphasis is put upon the brain (our mind), and our ability to think and reason. Not nearly enough emphasis is put on our heart, the core of our being where belief and faith grows (i.e. our spirit). When we over-emphasize our minds at the expense of our spirits, we lose that vital connection that God put within us that makes us "run."

In our physical body, the brain is dependent upon the heart for survival. The flow of blood to the brain makes it function the way God intended. The same holds true in our spirit. Our spirit is the center of who we are and should supply the necessary power and strength to the rest of our being. But, when the mind becomes the focus and center of who we are the correct connection is lost.... in essence, the heart is disconnected from the head. The result? A walking dead man!

Our brain and mind are not the center of who we are. People who live out of "their head" and not out of "their heart" are not functioning the way God intended. Life comes from the heart and from the spirit within. The head (mind, brain) can receive life from the heart but it has no ability to give life. This is why you can tell when somebody is "speaking from their head" versus "speaking from their heart." Life is imparted when someone speaks from their heart - you can sense it. So remember, your brain (mind) is built to be a responder to your heart... don't get that turned around.

Proverbs 3:5-6
Trust in the Lord with all thine HEART; and lean not unto thine own understanding [BRAIN, MIND].

TODAY'S FOOD FOR THOUGHT
Religion says, "YOU must make a sacrifice to be pleasing to God."
Christianity says, "CHRIST made a sacrifice for you to be pleasing to God."

6:33
June 30 | December 28

Sometimes God doesn't even have to say a word… sometimes it's a number! In my case the number is 6:33. I can't tell you how many times in a week I look at the clock only to find out that it's exactly 6:33. Dozens of times a month I see this number/time on my cell phone and my clock at home and without speaking a single word God says something to me… "Seek first the kingdom of God and His righteousness, and all these things will be added unto you" (Matthew 6:33). Others may think that it's just a strange coincidence, but I know better.

There are times when I have been struggling and worrying about things that were beyond my control, then I looked over at the clock to see "6:33." That little reminder tells me to stop worrying and to seek God's kingdom instead. At times I've been loaded down with the cares of life, distracted from what's really important, only to look down at my cell phone to check the time and read those numbers once again… "6:33." It whips my thinking back into line, and the distracting cares of life take a back seat to my pursuit of God's kingdom and His righteousness.

If you are struggling today with worry and the cares of this life God has a word for you… and it's really a number… 6:33. Have a blessed day today as you put God's things first.

A PLACE I NEVER LOOK

People who want to move FORWARD can't waste their time looking BEHIND them. In Luke 9:62, Jesus told us that people who are always looking behind them are not "fit" for the kingdom of God. With this idea in mind it's easy to see why Jesus rebuked the devil by saying, "Get thee BEHIND me, Satan!" Yes, the believer who addresses the devil in this manner is really saying, "Go to a place where I never look… BEHIND ME!"

Philippians 3:13 (NIV)
Brothers and sisters, I do not consider myself yet to have taken hold of it. But one thing I do: Forgetting what is BEHIND and straining toward what is ahead….

YOUR SMILE FOR TODAY
When Miss Taken and Miss Informed get together it won't be long before Miss Understanding shows up.

THE WORD "LIFE"
December 29

The word "LIFE" is an interesting word. Within its four letters 3 words can be found.

It contains the word "I"... the person who will determine how good or how bad LIFE will be for me. No one else has the same power over my life as "I" have.

It contains the word "IF"... which suggests that everything in LIFE is not "preset," but that outcomes will be determined by the decisions that I make when I'm given choices. IF I do right, I'll be blessed... IF I do wrong, I won't.

It also contains the word "LIE"... something I must avoid at all costs in LIFE in order to live in integrity and be free from the bondage of deception and that which is falsely proclaimed as truth.

LIFE is not always easy. There are "IFs" and "LIEs" in it. So "I" must be careful to live LIFE as God intended, taking responsibility for my own decisions and actions, and seeking the truth on every turn. Yes, this is when LIFE is at its very best.

JESUS LOVES YOU

I was reading the Bible one night and stumbled upon this verse:

"Now Jesus LOVED Martha, and her sister, and Lazarus." - John 11:5

For some reason that verse jumped off the page at me. Maybe it's because I've grown so accustomed to the idea that God loves THE WORLD that I've somehow forgotten that He loves INDIVIDUALS. Jesus is not like a rock star, singing on a stage for thousands, and loving them as a crowd but keeping a bodyguard between himself and adoring fans... individuals that the star really has no time for. Jesus LOVES individuals... JESUS LOVES YOU! Just thought you might like to hear that today!

TODAY'S WORD OF EXHORTATION
If it seems like you're at the end of your rope tie a "NOT" in it and say:
"This is NOT the end. God will NOT fail me. I can NOT be defeated. I will NOT give up. I am NOT a quitter. The devil will NOT win!"
"The LORD is on my side; I will NOT fear." Psalm 118:6

OUR EARS: THE "MOUTHS" OF OUR SPIRIT
December 30

I was trying to convey to my kids at church the importance of feeding our soul and spirit. Oftentimes we neglect the feeding of our soul and spirit, or, worse yet, feed them with very "unhealthy foods." I asked the kids, "How do we feed our bodies?" They answered, "By eating food with our mouths." So, I replied, "But how do you think we feed our souls and spirits?" They were puzzled. I said, "We feed our souls and spirits with our ears, through the things we hear... I guess you could say that our ears are the 'mouths of our spirits'". When I said that, one little boy grabbed his ear and pressed the top of his ear to the bottom of his ear in a "chomping" motion, like a mouth eating food. "Yes," I said, "That's right. When we're listening to words spoken, sung, or written it's just like our ears are chomping on food and the words are going into our soul and spirit for nourishment." I then had all the kids do the chomping motion with their ears that the one little boy had done. It was the perfect illustration for their young minds to understand (and it might help some "older" minds as well).

You know, we hear both good and bad, encouraging and discouraging words all day long. Just as healthy food makes our bodies stronger and unhealthy foods make us weak and sickly, the same holds true for the "food" that our souls and spirits feed on... the words we listen to, both intentionally and subconsciously. Our ears are the feeding stations of our spirit. We need to monitor what we listen to, and make sure that we're "feeding" our soul and spirit with healthy food... not junk food, or worse yet, poison! I like what I heard one person say, "My ears are not your garbage cans." Refuse to listen to "junk" that people try to push on you and poison you with. Remember that your ears are passageways into your soul and spirit, and should be protected.

My Prayer for Today:
"Lord, help me pay closer attention to the things I listen to as I realize that my spirit is feeding on the words I hear."

Luke 8:18
"So pay attention to how you hear. To those who listen to my teaching, more understanding will be given. But for those who are not listening, even what they think they understand will be taken away from them."

Romans 10:17
So then faith cometh by hearing, and hearing by the word of God.

HOW A MIRACLE HAPPENS
December 31

The Christmas story started 9 months before Jesus' birth in Bethlehem, when an angel came to a young girl named Mary and told her that she would become a mother, even though she was a virgin. Mary asked a simple question in response to this announcement, "How can this be since I am a virgin." In other words, "How will this miracle happen?" The angel answered her with a detailed description of how the miracle will take place when He said, *"The Holy Ghost shall come upon you, and the power of the Highest shall overshadow you...."* There you have it in a nutshell... how a miracle happens... how every miracle happens... not just for Mary, but for you and me also. Just two things need to happen.

FIRST, the Holy Spirit must "come upon" the situation (an empty womb, a diseased body, an insurmountable obstacle, etc.). Yes, something must first happen in the Spirit realm before anything is seen in this fleshly, natural realm. Just because you can't SEE it yet doesn't mean it's not happening. Mary was pregnant the moment that the Holy Spirit came upon her, but it wasn't until 9 months later that the promised baby boy became VISIBLE for all to see. You think that you haven't received your miracle just because you haven't SEEN it yet? Ha!

SECONDLY, the Power of the Most High overshadows the situation. Power is the energy that is emitted from God that makes the miracle happen. Everyone wants to feel the "power" when they pray for a miracle, but it's so important to remember that "first things must come first". The Holy Spirit has to "come upon" before the "power" is released.

In the story of Creation we all remember that God SPOKE and said, "Let there be light" and then power was emitted that created the light. But do you remember what was happening before that power went forth... before God spoke? Genesis 1:2 says, "And the Spirit of God was hovering over the waters." You see, before the miracle of Creation started, the Holy Spirit "came upon" the situation first!

So, this is just some encouragement to all who are praying for a miracle to happen. Pray for the miracle, then trust and wait for the Holy Spirit to COME UPON the situation to do His work in that unseen realm... that realm where ground work and preparation work is done before the Power is released and the miracle becomes visible for all to see.

2 Corinthians 5:7 - For we walk by faith, not by sight.

190

WHAT A SACRIFICE!

We think we comprehend the magnitude of Jesus' sacrifice when He died for us on the cross. But there was another sacrifice He made, before the cross, that we often overlook. Philippians 2:7 says when Jesus came to Earth that he "EMPTIED HIMSELF" and took on the form of a servant and became a man. Do we fully comprehend and appreciate this sacrifice… that He EMPTIED HIMSELF?

Consider this:

1. The God of Heaven, Who was "Everywhere present" and who "dwells in unapproachable light" was confined for nine months within the cramped, dark womb of a young virgin girl…WHAT A SACRIFICE!

2. The King of the Universe who sat upon a Heavenly throne with angels continually at his beck and call came to earth and was born in a BARN and wrapped up, not in royal garments, but in swaddling clothes (i.e. "rags")… WHAT A SACRIFICE!

3. As a child, the One who was called the "Everlasting Father" submitted himself to two earthly parents… good people no doubt, but still marred with human imperfections, so unlike Himself… WHAT A SACRIFICE!

4. The God who said in Psalm 50:12 "If I were hungry I wouldn't tell you" became a man who hungered and thirsted during His forty day fast in the wilderness… WHAT A SACRIFICE!

5. The God who "never slumbers or sleeps" became a man who got tired and needed rest. He was so tired on one occasion that he slept in a boat that was being tossed about in a storm, (wind blowing and waves splashing in His face) and would not have awakened if the disciples hadn't pressured him to get up… WHAT A SACRIFICE!

6. The One who came from Heaven, a place where there are no tears or sorrow, came to Earth to be known as the MAN OF SORROWS ACQUAINTED WITH GRIEF. He did not know what tears were in Heaven but He experienced them at the grave of Lazarus…WHAT A SACRIFICE!

This is only a short list of the great sacrifices that Jesus made when He emptied himself to become a man. And you thought the only sacrifice He made was when He died on the cross!